Discovering
a Sermon

Discovering
a Sermon
Personal Pastoral Preaching

Robert C. Dykstra

CHALICE
PRESS
ST. LOUIS, MISSOURI

Cover art and design: Michael Foley
Interior design: Elizabeth Wright
Art direction: Michael Domínguez

This book is printed on acid-free, recycled paper.

Visit Chalice Press on the World Wide Web at
www.chalicepress.com

10 9 8 7 6 5 4 3 2   03

Library of Congress Cataloging–in–Publication Data
Dykstra, Robert C., 1956-
    Discovering a sermon : personal pastoral preaching / Robert C. Dykstra
        p.   cm.
    ISBN 0-8272-0627-5
    1. Preaching   I. Title.
BV4211.3 .D95 2001
251 – dc21   2001004595
                                                              CIP

Printed in the United States of America

For Molly,
content and craving contentment

I am content with what I have,
Little be it or much;
And, Lord, contentment still I crave,
Because thou savest such.

JOHN BUNYAN
from "The Shepherd's Song"
Pilgrim's Progress

Contents

Acknowledgments

I wish to thank Donald Capps, my mentor, friend, and colleague in pastoral theology at Princeton Theological Seminary, for the countless ways that he has encouraged me over the years and for his generous suggestions for enhancing this book. Don embodies an ideal of personal modesty and professional generativity—of grace and works—to which I can only continue to aspire. I am grateful, too, to Jon L. Berquist, my editor at Chalice Press, for supporting this project from the outset and for his steady guidance, patience, and good cheer in seeing it through to its conclusion. I also trust that those pastors who participated in my continuing education seminars on pastoral preaching at the University of Dubuque Theological Seminary, the Toronto School of Theology, and Princeton Theological Seminary will recognize their own creative imprints on the book. I honor here as well the memory of my parents who, by their own unassuming witness, first introduced me to Jesus Christ and so gave me reason to preach. Finally, I dedicate this book to my wife, Molly, who amazed me as I wrote in giving birth to our daughter, Eleanor, and who continues to astonish me daily with her kindness, beauty, serenity, and longing.

Introduction

The congregation with which I worship gathers on uncomfortable pews in an old clapboard church building surrounded by a historic cemetery with worn and faded tombstones. At a particular point in our service each Sunday, young children are dismissed who wish to attend a special worship education activity, and in order to reach their classroom, they must walk outside around the perimeter of the graveyard. On a recent Sunday morning shortly after they left the worship service, I happened to glance out the sanctuary windows and saw the children walking in the distance beyond the cemetery.

I had witnessed a similar scene, of course, through the same windows on previous occasions. This time, however, something about those children walking past the gravestones captured my attention as significant or potentially so, as if I were at last seeing them for the first time. The easy proximity of unassuming young lives to the shadow of death unsettled me for a moment before my thoughts returned inside to the minister reading the morning scripture lesson.

This book seeks to describe how so ordinary a diversion as this often comes to be the occupational hazard, but also rich reward, of pastoral preaching, hinting simultaneously at the threatening absence and alluring presence of God. Pastoral preaching involves, above all, paying attention and taking notice. "The first criterion of success in any human activity," wrote W. H. Auden, "the necessary preliminary, whether to scientific discovery or to artistic vision, is intensity of attention or, less

1

pompously, love,"[1] an intensity of attention no less essential to nuanced pastoral preaching than to other creative endeavors.

But attention to what? Faced with pressing demands and many distractions, where does the preacher focus her gaze or direct his concentration? More crassly, how does one discern that an image, text, or event might "preach," and not only *might* preach but that, like the message of a powerful dream, *insists* on being preached, *must* be preached? What in the sudden association of children and graveyard captured my attention earlier and continues to linger still? What constitutes its potential to disturb and redeem?

Such questions lead to even further questions concerning the nature of practical theology and practical knowledge, that complex realm of knowing that includes preaching and pastoral care as well as many other tasks of ministry and life not easily put to words or gathered from books. How, indeed, does one learn to play baseball or paint landscapes, to cultivate land or perform neurosurgery? Individuals do somehow come to master these skills, not likely first without what Auden calls intensity of attention or love, but then usually a love carefully constrained and honed under the watchful eye of a mentor or community. For all preaching generally, but for pastoral preaching specifically, the question becomes then not only to which of the myriad voices we intensely attend but to what crucible or clan we submit that attention for refinement and nurture.

These questions resist easy answers. One straightforward way to begin, oddly, may be to avoid addressing them at all, or rather to begin less by attempting to answer them than by attending to whatever answers happen to present themselves to us. O. K. Bouwsma tells of a conversation with fellow philosopher Ludwig Wittgenstein concerning a third-rate play that Wittgenstein had seen years earlier at the age of twenty-two:

> One detail in that play had made a powerful impression upon him. It was a trifle. But here some peasant, some ne'er-do-well says in the play: "Nothing can hurt me." That remark went through [Wittgenstein] and now he remembers it. It started things. You can't tell. The most important things just happen to you.[2]

Our intentional efforts to make something important happen—to make ourselves fall in love, say, or even to preach a riveting sermon—often prove futile and detract from those unexpected trifles that bear far more potential for our hopes of intimacy or for tasks of proclamation. Why not begin instead by attending to what of interest just happens to us or by contemplating what intrigues us?

One reason against the "Why not?", a complication of this promising starting point, is the ease with which adults in general— and perhaps ministers in particular—come to disregard or even cease to recognize what interests them. This loss of interest at times stems from painful childhood deprivations, but also more inevitably from cultural or religious conventions that equate maturity with relinquishing desire, and more expressly with renouncing childhood fascination with bodies and their many pleasures. "Children want to know about sexuality," writes British child psychoanalyst Adam Phillips, paraphrasing Freud.

> But grown-ups tell them they need to know about something else; and they need to know about something else—call it culture—to distract them from what they are really interested in. Education, Freud implies, teaches the child either to lose interest in what matters most to her or to compromise her interest. Interest has to have something added to it, called education, to make it acceptable.[3]

Development, particularly moral or spiritual development, has often assumed a disavowal of one's desires along with surrendering any claims to being interested in oneself or of being worthy of the interest of others.

Ministers tend to have excelled in these early lessons and have learned to pride themselves on distrusting what interests them, most notably things "of the flesh" that once captured their attention as children. However, this process of segregating or splitting off one's interests and desires, for its considerable social and ecclesiastical benefits, exacts certain costs as well, not least for our purposes, the preacher's becoming less interesting for being less authentically human. Frederick Buechner writes:

Sad to say, the people who seem to lose touch with themselves...most conspicuously are of all things ministers...I don't say they do it more than other people but they do it more publicly...[A] major part of their ministry is to remind us that there is nothing more important than to pay attention to what is happening to us, yet again and again they show little sign of doing so themselves. There is precious little in most of their preaching to suggest that they have rejoiced and suffered with the rest of mankind. If they draw on their own experience at all, it is usually for some little anecdote to illustrate a point or help make the pill go down but rarely if ever for an authentic, first-hand, flesh-and-blood account of what it is like to love Christ, say, or to feel spiritually bankrupt, or to get fed up with the whole religious enterprise.[4]

The organic relation of interest to vitality, of what excites the preacher's own passions to what is urgently proclaimed from the pulpit, of what one attends to and desires, to what one confesses to be redemptive and true, is somehow severed or lost.

Adam Phillips, from his psychological perspective, similarly links interest to health and well-being. He conceives of psychotherapy as a process for reclaiming lost curiosity that, in turn, engenders embryonic hope: "So one of the aims of analysis is to free people to do nothing to the future but be interested in it...Only our surprises—and those less inviting surprises called traumas—can sabotage our foregone conclusions."[5]

The therapeutic sabotage that Phillips attributes to psychoanalysis aptly characterizes as well the mission of one who preaches of Jesus Christ and the God of the biblical witness. The primary burden of the preacher who speaks on behalf of this divine Saboteur of foregone conclusions becomes, then, less one of being interesting than of being interested, of doing nothing to the future but being interested in it. As Jürgen Moltmann states, "[H]uman existence or being (*esse*) is being interested (*interesse*)."[6] It follows, then, that a sudden association like mine of children and graveyard may well signal pangs of healing or transformation—the unsettling distraction a potential harbinger of hope or trauma enough to sabotage foregone conclusions.

Before the first word is pronounced from the pulpit, the preacher must be caught unawares, must take a hint or follow a lead, keenly attuning to those most important trifles that just happen to happen and that contain power to undermine the inevitable. The preacher, in other words, must become like a little child, at least in terms of recovering a child's insatiable curiosity and appetite for life and of reclaiming a child's bold assumption of entitlement to the interest of others.

Intensity of attention, then, above eloquence of expression, wordless silence prior to articulate speech, modest listening before wise counsel, solitary voyeurism over public exhibitionism; these constitute the loving preliminaries not only for creative achievement but for life itself. Together they appear remarkably reminiscent of the preverbal competencies—or from an adult perspective, the incompetencies—of infancy. Attention, silence, listening, and voyeurism all variously describe regression to an original muteness that is precursor to spirited pastoral preaching.

Pursuing the Enticing Lead

Seminarians and seasoned pastors alike sometimes comment on the tensions between their ministries of preaching and pastoral care, rightly noting that these two tasks require seemingly contradictory ways of approaching or communicating with their parishioners. From this perspective, incongruities between the assumptions and methods of preaching and of pastoral care could conspire to make "pastoral preaching" little more than an oxymoron. Even while acknowledging these discrepancies, however, other ministers would hesitate to draw too sharp a distinction between two responsibilities so integral to their calling. From this second perspective, the sheer fact that most sermons are delivered by pastors alert to the joys, sorrows, and needs of their congregations lends credence to the claim that virtually all preaching is pastoral preaching. Still others would call for a third, more moderate position, considering pastoral preaching a specifically topical approach that seeks to offer discernment for those struggling with timely pastoral concerns such as grief, addiction, sexuality, divorce, or euthanasia.[7]

Although collectively difficult to reconcile, each of these positions—whether conceiving of pastoral preaching as nearly impossible, as virtually inevitable, or as primarily topical—holds considerable individual merit. The differences in communication styles between preaching and pastoral care are not easily resolved, yet preachers typically do strive to weigh the pastoral needs of their parishioners and, at times, use topical sermons to good effect as one means of addressing those concerns.

However, while recognizing and even affirming the value of these various perspectives, I see pastoral preaching somewhat differently, certainly as neither impossible, inevitable, nor even topical. Pastoral preaching, I submit, is distinguished less by the communicational style or skill of the person in the pulpit, less by sensitivity to deep concerns in the pews, less by focusing on particularly pressing issues of the day, however pivotal each of these may be to the preaching event. Pastoral preaching is distinctly marked, rather, by the pastor's personal willingness to pursue enticing leads peculiar to every biblical text or human circumstance that allude to the divine preoccupation with happy endings amid human tragedy. "We proclaim Christ crucified, a stumbling block to Jews and foolishness to Gentiles" is the apostle Paul's perhaps more direct way of putting it (1 Cor. 1:23). Rich pastoral preaching no doubt entails much more than this but insists on nothing less; it is contingent not on a giftedness for speech but on intensity of attention and love.

A Ministry of Absence

To attempt to return as adults to this kind of primal attentiveness and expectancy takes a certain measure of courage. Beyond the more obvious temerity necessary for speaking before others some word of understanding in frequently ambiguous situations, a preacher also needs formidable courage simply to be alone. Sermons delivered in public are conceived and gestate in private; the cordiality of the pastor on Sunday veils the desolation of Monday. Preaching is solitary work, and to the extent that the preacher as a person has developed, in the words of psychoanalyst D. W. Winnicott, the capacity to be alone, she or he will have something of meaning to say from the pulpit before others.[8]

James O. Freedman, the shy and esteemed most recent past president of Dartmouth, raised eyebrows but also eventually the intellectual ethos of the college by suggesting in his 1987 inaugural address, "We must strengthen our attraction for those singular students whose greatest pleasures may come not from the camaraderie of classmates, but from the lonely acts of writing poetry or mastering the cello or solving mathematical riddles or translating Catullus."[9] That Freedman's encouraging sequestered scholarship seemed, at the time, a radical proposal to a distinguished university audience is no less telling than that a plea for solitude appears increasingly suspect in ministry as well. How sadly difficult to imagine the church, with Dartmouth, seeking out shy and reclusive leaders who, lacking the conviviality so valued by congregations, found no greater pleasure than in solitary acts of following and only subsequently confiding where their childlike, even childish, intensity of attention—their love— would lead.

Pastoral work clearly requires a certain camaraderie of classmates along with discretion and skill in a ministry of presence; these social demands and abilities, however, are sustained by an equally insistent ministry of absence, by the capacity to be alone. For their many important differences, preaching and pastoral care unite in pastoral preaching in asking of the minister considerable personal courage and risk—the courage not only to speak but to remain silent, the risk of vulnerability before others but not least of being alone.

Naming the Peculiar

Silence and solitude open a space for preachers to reclaim childlike curiosity, to dare to name once again what they want, to acknowledge, if only to themselves, and to trust, if only for a time, their thoughts, daydreams, doubts, and longings, including even undesirable desires of body and soul. Ralph Waldo Emerson once remarked:

> When I attended church, and the man in the pulpit was all clay and not of tuneable metal, I thought that if men would avoid that general language and general manner in which they strive to hide all that is peculiar, and would

say only what was uppermost in their own minds, after
their own individual manner, every man would be
interesting.[10]

In shielding themselves less from all things particular, Emerson
was saying, preachers paradoxically may touch more on things
universal.

However refreshing Emerson's plea, does not his calling
preachers to a degree of personal candor also threaten to invite
narcissistic excess? Would not our urging preachers to follow
their interests only heighten the immodesty already inherent in
speaking anything of God to others? Do not boorish preachers
who hide behind their openness, or grandiose others who radiate
self-assurance, provide ample cause for restraint in matters of
the heart?

While my own Reformed predispositions would ordinarily
lead me to echo these very concerns, they have less force for
me in this instance, for I sense that the vulnerability or bravado
of preachers often betrays not an excess, but a lack of self-
awareness. Their posturing arises not out of but over against the
silence and solitude that I advocate here. Preachers who speak
only *about* their own yearnings become themselves the main
point; those who instead speak *from* or *out of* their yearnings
attempt to convey, as the eucharistic prayer attests, One "unto
whom all hearts are open, all desires known, and from whom
no secrets are hid."[11] A fine but significant line separates these
demeanors, the latter more modest witness expressing my hope
for pastoral preaching. We may recall that in early Christian
preaching, Jesus' own disciples told of no less than an unsettling
singularity that just happened to them, that captured their minds,
consumed their passions, and wholly sabotaged their foregone
conclusions. The crucified and risen Christ was sufficient hedge
against excessive homiletic self-concern.

A Clandestine Shame in Sermons

Authors of texts on preaching typically apologize for
including, usually near the end of the book, one or more of their
own sermons. They reveal that the decision to incorporate the
sermons involved much personal consternation or, strangely,

that the sermons are not meant to be models or in any way exemplary. They also caution that sermons are to be heard, not read, and therefore may appear limp or lifeless on the printed page.

However sincerely intended, such disclaimers strike me as at least puzzling and possibly also misguided. This consistent reticence to include their own sermons in all likelihood has little to do with the quality of the published sermons, which I assume that most authors, usually accomplished preachers themselves, consider to represent their best work. It probably has even less to do with any difference between the spoken and written word, a distinction that readers easily appreciate and accommodate.

Their recurring reluctance points instead to a sense of shame that accompanies every sermon regardless of its quality, whether published or preached. Any sermon publicly exposes, if only covertly, nuances of the preacher's intimate encounters with God and others, making sermons intrinsically, often unwittingly, self-revealing and therefore shaming for the preacher. Even without explicit personal reference, a preacher can feel naked before others in the sermon, which may also help to explain a subtle temptation to shame one's listeners in kind ("What's good for the goose is good for the gander"). Authors and preachers alike who denigrate their own sermons may be struggling to articulate this shame that is endemic not to the preacher or the listener, but to the revelatory nature of sermons themselves.

One learns *what* to preach in large measure through sustained attention to one's interests and desires; one learns *how* to preach in large measure through imitating others. Like case studies or verbatims in my primary field of pastoral care and counseling, sermons function within homiletics texts to model a particular style or approach. Thus, the sermons included here are found not only at the end but throughout the book. This will spare readers the effort of investing in a theory of preaching whose tangible fruits are deferred indefinitely, but will also ensure that this exploration through new terrain remains consistently grounded in actual practice.

Each of the following chapters centers on one of my own sermons that exemplifies this book's approach to pastoral preaching and that together form its theological core. I assume that not every sermon nor the collective style will interest or appeal to every reader, but I do hope to convey that these sermons interest and appeal to, yet also disclose and consequently shame, their author.

Looking Ahead

This book is intended for experienced pastors seeking to recover something of their original wonder in preaching but also as a primer for seminarians and others new to pastoral preaching. It introduces a model of sermon preparation that concentrates especially on connecting biblical texts with contemporary life and, foremost, with the preacher's own experiences in life. This happens in part through a process of creating contemporary parables whereby discrepant associations—such as mine of children and the graveyard—are brought to bear on a given passage of scripture. Here, the preacher redirects that energy previously expended in searching out anecdotal illustrations to more satisfying pastoral and homiletical ends.

Each of the first four chapters initially introduces a key theme or aspect of pastoral preaching, offers an actual sermon that exemplifies the model as a whole, and concludes with an analysis of the sermon in terms of the initial theme. Chapter 1 focuses on biblical exegesis in light of Winnicott's observations concerning a child's capacity to be alone. Chapter 2 examines the exegesis of stories from contemporary life, enlisting Adam Phillips, a disciple of Winnicott, as an atypical homiletical mentor for reclaiming lost curiosity. Chapter 3 emphasizes listening in community, inviting scrutiny by a company of strangers of any emerging interpretation of the biblical texts and stories from life. Chapter 4 presents the parabolic process whereby new liaisons are forged between the holy and the mundane and outlines additional basic principles for weaving these various strands into a satisfying whole. An epilogue breaks rank with this pattern by offering one final sermon that pursues my recent sighting of children in a graveyard.

CHAPTER 1

Playing with the Text

In informal conversation following an address to a group of young Anglican clergy just months before his death in 1971, British psychoanalyst D. W. Winnicott was asked for guidance in distinguishing troubled parishioners who could be helped by pastoral conversation alone from those who needed to be referred to a psychiatrist for assistance. Winnicott later told a colleague "that he had been taken aback by the awesome simplicity" of this question, and that after pausing for a long while, he had responded to the ministers by saying, "If a person comes and talks to you and, listening to him, you feel he is *boring* you, then he is sick, and needs psychiatric treatment. But if he sustains your interest, no matter how grave his distress or conflict, then you can help him alright."[1] Being boring, Winnicott determined, signified emotional distress severe enough to warrant further intervention.

Beyond its benefit for pastoral counseling, Winnicott's insight concerning the diagnostic value of boredom may prove equally on the mark for our present concern with pastoral preaching, though with a distinctive turn. In preaching, the roles sometimes become reversed, with preachers less in the position of the counselor than of the counselee, of the one experienced as boring.

If it is too often the case today that those who hear sermons find them less than interesting, would it not be conceivable, given Winnicott's criterion for relative psychological health, that such sermons reflect a certain severity of emotional or spiritual discord in those who preach?

Masud Khan, the colleague whom Winnicott later told of the clergy's concern, suggests that Winnicott's response makes explicit near the end of his life a thematic thread that actually spans many earlier decades of his writings as a practicing pediatrician and psychoanalyst.[2] In tracing this thread, however, Khan points out that Winnicott sharply distinguishes between a person who is *boring* and one who is *bored*. To bore others, as Winnicott's response to the clergy makes clear, is to betray an intensity of psychological distress, whereas to *be* bored is instead an ordinary, even necessary, and oddly desirable part of everyday life. For Winnicott the capacity to be bored—closely linked to what he calls the capacity to be alone—reflects a welcome developmental achievement and a sign of psychological health. Indeed, the capacity to be bored may serve as something of an antidote to the emotional terror hidden in the act of being boring. Put differently, preachers whose sermons are found to be boring may well be those very preachers, often through circumstances beyond their choosing, sadly incapable of being bored.

This chapter initially explores findings from Winnicott's psychoanalytic observations of infants and toddlers in seeking to understand how ministers may find themselves subtly pressured to become boring and how their underlying fears of boredom may be exposed, diminished, and ultimately overcome. Winnicott's work makes a case for helping preachers to become less boring not by encouraging flamboyance or by compelling interest, but paradoxically by enhancing their capacity to be bored and, more specifically I will argue, their capacity to be bored with any particular biblical text.

Preparing for the Word

Donald Woods Winnicott was born in 1896, in Plymouth, England, to a prominent and, according to Winnicott, "preoccupied" businessman father twice elected mayor of the city and an idealized, but more opaque, and sometimes inconsolably depressed mother. The family was Wesleyan Methodist, and throughout his life Winnicott strove to emulate Wesley's use of plain language to make his work accessible. As an adolescent, Winnicott eventually converted to the Anglican church while attending boarding school in Cambridge. At twenty-four, with a natural rapport with young children and adolescents and described by friends as the life of the party, Winnicott became a physician specializing in children's medicine. Newly captivated by Freud's writings, he was analyzed during this same period by James Strachey and Joan Riviere, two noted therapists themselves analyzed by Freud. Through decades as a keen observer of relationships between children and their mothers and in writing scores of articles eventually gathered into more than a dozen books, Winnicott came to prominence as a chief proponent of a distinctively British variation of psychoanalysis known as object relations theory.[3]

Truth Created and Found

One of Winnicott's clinical innovations, which he called "the spatula game,"[4] captures something of the spirit of object relations theory and of Winnicott's understanding of how psychotherapy heals; it also hints at how being *boring* came, for him, to represent the height of psychological disorder while being *bored* became a welcome invitation to discovering authentic desire.

In the spatula game Winnicott asks that a mother in consultation sit opposite him "with the angle of the table coming between me and her" and with the baby on her knee: "As a routine I place a right-angled shining tongue-depressor at the edge of the table and I invite the mother to place the child in such a way that, if the child should wish to handle the spatula, it is possible." Winnicott then observes how the infant responds to this invitation:

> Stage 1. The baby puts his hand to the spatula, but at this moment discovers unexpectedly that the situation must be given thought. He is in a fix. Either with his hand resting on the spatula and his body quite still he looks at me and his mother with big eyes, and watches

and waits, or, in certain cases, he withdraws interest completely and buries his face in the front of the mother's blouse. It is usually possible to manage the situation so that active reassurance is not given, and it is very interesting to watch the gradual and spontaneous return of the child's interest in the spatula.

Stage 2. All the time, in "the period of hesitation" (as I call it), the baby holds his body still (but not rigid). Gradually he becomes brave enough to let his feelings develop, and then the picture changes quite quickly. The moment at which this first phase changes into the second is evident, for the child's acceptance of the reality of desire for the spatula is heralded by a change in the inside of the mouth, which becomes flabby, while the tongue looks thick and soft, and saliva flows copiously. Before long he puts the spatula into his mouth and is chewing it with his gums, or seems to be copying father smoking a pipe. The change in the baby's behaviour is a striking feature. Instead of expectancy and stillness there now develops self-confidence, and there is free bodily movement, the latter related to the manipulation of the spatula.

I have frequently made the experiment of trying to get the spatula to the infant's mouth during the stage of hesitation. [I]t is impossible during this stage to [accomplish this] apart from the exercise of brutal strength. In certain cases where the inhibition is acute any effort on my part that results in the spatula being moved towards the child produces screaming, mental distress, or actual colic.

The baby now seems to feel that the spatula is in his possession, perhaps in his power, certainly available for the purposes of self-expression.[5]

This little exercise attests to Winnicott's conviction that the discovery of spontaneous personal desire arises in an optimally secure and inviting setting, a "holding environment,"[6] and cannot be imposed or coerced by another without ill effect.

Even as an infant has no conception that the breast which nourishes her arises not out of her own powerful desires but from the loving provision of her mother, so too the infant conceives of the spatula, in reality made available by another, as somehow the product of her own striving, and her desire for it perceived as stemming spontaneously from within her own body or self. In order to grow in self-confidence and expressiveness, the infant needs this illusion to be maintained, needs first to discover, indeed to create, her desire for the proffered spatula. To have such desire imposed on her leads only to distress and torment or, even worse for Winnicott, to compliance and the development of a false self whose function, in part, is to care for her caretakers. The infant sacrifices her legitimate need to be cared for by others in having instead to care for them.

Similarly, the healing power of psychotherapy, for Winnicott, derives less from insightful, and never from forced, interpretations by the therapist than from the "potential space," the realm of shared illusion, between therapist and patient. Adam Phillips writes:

> [F]or Winnicott the mother-infant relationship, in which communication was relatively non-verbal, had become the paradigm for the analytic process, and this changed the role of interpretation in psychoanalytic treatment... "What matters to the patient," [Winnicott] writes,... "is not the accuracy of the interpretation so much as the willingness of the analyst to help, the analyst's capacity to identify with the patient and so to believe in what is needed and to meet the need as soon as the need is indicated verbally or in non-verbal or pre-verbal language."[7]

This often silent space between therapist and patient allows for the surprising arousal of spontaneous desire within the patient; though provided in large part by the concern and relational skill of the therapist, this space is likewise necessarily discovered and shaped by each individual patient. A holding environment, whether of mother for child or of therapist for patient, makes provision without coercion; it intrigues and entices without compulsion to compliance. In interpreting Winnicott, James W. Jones writes:

> Knowledge arises neither from the external world impressing itself on our passive minds nor from the projection of our subjective ideas onto a blank screen. Rather, "understanding emerges from interaction, from constant negotiation with the environment and other people." Or, in Winnicott's more vivid language, truth is both "created and found."[8]

Holding and Biblical Interpretation

The spatula game can serve as a parable of sorts in linking Winnicott's psychology to pastoral preaching. Given the complexities of the preaching task, one could envision the preacher taking the role of nearly any of the various players in the spatula game, including the spatula itself! Perhaps most promising in terms of the earliest stages of sermon preparation—what to do with the biblical text—would be to configure the preacher in the role of the infant on the lap of its mother, here the church and its traditions, with God or Jesus in place of the analyst, and with any particular biblical passage in the position of the spatula. Given this scenario, one could argue that vitality in preaching springs from the preacher's discovering a specific biblical text on his or her own terms amid the watchful—and tempering—presence of God and the church.

Like the spatula, the biblical text is placed by others within the grasp of the preacher. From this perspective the preacher often does not choose the text that forms the dynamic core of a sermon. Instead, the inspiration of God, we say, and some ancient and usually anonymous persons of faith have provided the text and its truth.

Winnicott's observations of infants in the spatula game, however, may qualify this objective reality by another more nuanced one, namely, that in making it decisively his or her own, the preacher spontaneously discovers, desires, grapples with, manipulates, "chews on," and in effect "creates" the very biblical text provided by others. In confronting a passage of scripture, the preacher, like the infant within range of a spatula, is "in a fix," on the one hand wanting to swallow, but on the other wanting to hide from the text. The preacher, too, watches and waits, at first withdrawing and burying her face in the church's "blouse," but gradually gaining enough courage to accept the reality of her desire for the text.

Unless preachers first allow themselves, and are allowed, the illusion of the text as the product of their own striving, no living word will likely emerge from it. Winnicott could neither impose the spatula on a hesitant child without emotional distress nor effectively force an interpretation on an adult in psychotherapy. So too a rendering of a biblical text compelled by tradition or orthodoxy, by recognized authorities or esteemed commentators of church or culture, or even by the preacher's own concerns for doing God's will or speaking God's word leads to a similarly unsatisfying outcome. As Winnicott sought to prevent a mother from prematurely reassuring her hesitant child concerning the spatula, one can imagine God seeking to restrain ecclesiastical or other powerful voices, including even God's own, from too swiftly prevailing in the preacher's initial encounter with a specific biblical text. Truth, Winnicott insists, and I would add even biblical truth, must be at once created and found.

This raises a very practical preliminary matter concerning use of the lectionary for selecting texts in preaching. Does the lectionary, a broadly disseminated list of biblical texts assigned to particular days, or the related *lectio continua* method of preaching through a single book of the Bible over a period of weeks, curtail in any way the preacher's personal discovery of or desire for the text?[9]

A case could be made here for caution, and I personally tend to use only one of the several assigned texts for the day in any given sermon. Yet I have found that the lectionary actually liberates the preacher more than it constricts, and I generally advocate such a method for selecting texts, including even in special circumstances of a wedding or funeral. The lectionary places a text within range of the preacher, not unlike the pediatrician or mother who places the spatula or another appealing object within reach of the infant; it establishes something of a holding environment without forcing one's hand. Both lectionary and *lectio continua* approaches make provision without coercion; they intrigue and entice without compulsion to compliance. Presuming neither the passivity of a preacher's own mind nor the ultimacy of a preacher's own concerns, the lectionary makes space for negotiation between self and other and often stimulates the exhilarating and paradoxical sense of truth as created and found.

A Necessary Illusion

Winnicott's conviction concerning the paradox of truth as created and found—emerging, as the spatula game reveals, from observations of infants with their mothers—is closely tied to that which became his most celebrated discovery: transitional phenomena or transitional objects. As infants of four-to-twelve months moved from an initial inability to distinguish themselves from others to an awareness of increasingly differentiated boundaries, Winnicott began to notice the significance to them of various prized objects or ritualized behaviors. A teddy bear, a particular doll, a special blanket, or a certain lullaby or established bedtime routine became especially soothing to them when anxious: "This object goes on being important. The parents get to know its value and carry it round when travelling. The mother lets it get dirty and even smelly, knowing that by washing it she introduces a break in the continuity of the infant's experience, a break that may destroy the meaning and value of the object to the infant."[10] The ordinary doll or blanket suddenly takes on religious import to the infant and mother alike, serving as a bridge and cushion, as a shared illusion, between them:

> I am here staking a claim for an intermediate state between a baby's inability and his growing ability to recognize and accept reality. I am therefore studying the substance of *illusion,* that which is allowed to the infant, and which in adult life is inherent in art and religion, and yet becomes the hallmark of madness when an adult puts too powerful a claim on the credulity of others, forcing them to acknowledge a sharing of illusion that is not their own.[11]

The teddy bear or soothing ritual thus becomes only the first in a lifelong series of intermediaries, eventually broadening in scope to include culture and religion, that unite but simultaneously differentiate inner and outer realms of personal experience. As a mother honors a particular transitional object or ritual without having to experience it precisely as her child does, so one person in a relationship allows for the religious experience of another without necessarily having personally shared it. Conversely, Winnicott notes that one can no more impose a transitional object on a child without damaging psychological consequences than, barring madness, one can compel others to claim as their own a unique religious vision or experience. The infant or the believer alone can establish the special worth of the object or experience, while the mother or an esteemed other, in turn, confirms its sacred status.

Given the pivotal role of transitional phenomena in Winnicott's psychology and my own desire to show their relevance for pastoral preaching, the specific qualities of a child's first "not-me" relationship are worth outlining in detail. Winnicott suggests that the infant assumes rights over the transitional object, and parents agree to this assumption, though the infant surrenders at least some omnipotence over the object from the outset. The infant affectionately cuddles the object but also excitedly loves and mutilates it. The object is to be changed only by the infant and must survive instinctual loving as well as hating and, if present, the infant's pure aggression. Yet it must seem to the infant to give warmth, move, or do something that demonstrates its own unique vitality. The object is perceived as originating neither from within nor from outside the infant's own self; it is not a hallucination. Eventually decreasing in emotional significance, the object finally is less forgotten than "relegated to limbo." It loses meaning, Winnicott believed, "because the transitional phenomena have become diffused, have become spread out over the whole intermediate territory between 'inner psychic reality' and 'the external world as perceived by two persons in common,' that is to say, over the whole cultural field."[12]

The "good-enough" mother or caretaker, according to Winnicott, initially adapts herself actively to her infant's every need and desire and thereby sustains the infant's illusory omnipotence. Gradually this original paradise must be lost, and the transitional object or phenomenon begins then to serve as an intersubjective intermediary between the infant and mother; the mother appropriately decreases her adaptation according to the infant's growing capacity to tolerate frustration. Without adequate prior "illusioning," however, this disillusioning process is doomed to fail.[13] Adam Phillips comments that initially,

> [t]he mother makes what is in fact a dialogue between her and her infant appear to him as a monologue born of his desire. By virtue of the mother's adaptation…there is an area of illusion; it is as though, from the infant's point of view, he creates in fantasy the mother he needs and finds. The infant, in Winnicott's account, discovers the world by first creating it; he is born an artist and a hedonist. Where Freud…had emphasized the role of disillusionment in human development, in which growing up was a process of mourning, for Winnicott there was a more primary sense in which development was a creative process of collaboration. Disillusionment presupposed sufficient illusionment. For the infant at the very beginning, given a holding environment, desire was creative rather than simply rapacious.[14]

Phillips reiterates Winnicott's claim that truth is both created and found, but also conveys his sense of the original goodness or graciousness of creation and human development. If Eden is only an illusion, it is for Winnicott a necessary illusion that alone suffices to sustain the child's developing self after its inevitable eviction from the garden.

Text as Object

In light of Winnicott's assertion that art and religion function for an adult much like a teddy bear for an infant, the scriptures come readily to mind as serving essentially as a transitional object for the preacher. Winnicott's insights into a child's rightful authority over a transitional object could be taken to prod preachers to approach a given biblical text with a certain corresponding air of omnipotence. Winnicott seems almost to insist that the ordered calm of the pastor's study become somehow transformed into the creative chaos of the artist's studio or the provocative allure of the hedonist's lair.

Granted, these rather grandiose images of pastor as biblical artisan or holy hedonist probably run contrary to the image that most ministers seek to groom, and, indeed, when communicated from the pulpit, an attitude of pastoral omnipotence almost invariably diminishes the impact of a sermon. In the privacy of his or her own study, however, as a minister first considers a particular biblical text, this infantile illusion of omnipotence seems somehow precisely appropriate. In private, the preacher can and even must approach the text with the authority and freedom of an infant with beloved teddy in tow, as if, at least for the moment, the dialogue between preacher and God or between preacher and church were instead a monologue born of the preacher's own desire.

Some may protest that this attitude of pastoral omnipotence would foster disrespect for sacred scripture and mitigate its authority and autonomy. I submit, however, that likening the biblical text to a transitional object actually enhances the preacher's esteem for the text. The text becomes an irreplaceable treasure, a coveted possession that must never be lost, "laundered," or otherwise altered by others. The preacher desires to be near it and to play with it. The text gains texture, provides warmth, and moves with a reality all its own; it singularly unites and differentiates ephemeral boundaries between the preacher's inner and outer realities, as well as between the preacher's secret hopes and fears and the often hidden life of God. The biblical text-as-object offers intimacy without invasion and individuality without isolation. The preacher's initial illusion of omnipotence over the text paradoxically ensures its sacred status. Exegesis begins in Eden.

The preacher, I am arguing, must first come to the text alone and on his or her own terms. With scholarly commentaries still on their shelves and sermon chat sessions with parishioners or others postponed to another day, the preacher and the text for now play alone together. In beginning to prepare for an upcoming sermon, this translates for me into simply photocopying the lectionary text or texts, grabbing a new yellow notepad, setting aside a two-hour block of time at the earliest possible opportunity, and sitting quietly with the text, free from outside interruptions. I attempt to find another hour or two to sit alone with the text again on the following day. I seek, in particular, a great freedom of access to the text during these times. Like the infant or toddler who at once loves and hates, cuddles and mutilates the teddy bear or blanket, so too I attempt to bring the full range of my love and hate, my naïveté and suspicion, my faith and doubt, my sexuality and soul, and my knowledge and ignorance to the text under scrutiny.

Winnicott noticed that in promoting a formerly subjective object to the status of a transitional object, the infant necessarily abrogated some omnipotence over it, in effect having to grant the newly embellished object an objective reality of its own. Similarly, in raising the stature of the biblical text to transitional object, the preacher abrogates a certain degree of power over it, acknowledging the text's own inherent integrity. Despite this abrogation, however, at this early stage the preacher must strive to temper those internal voices that would discourage careful scrutiny of the biblical text. The preacher attempts to check any personal tendency to censor particular questions, thoughts, doubts, associations, or concerns that may seem awkward or even shameful to put to an esteemed and holy authority. Instead, the preacher as artist and hedonist strives to retain authority over the text by subjecting it to seemingly arcane or outrageous questions and concerns. To succumb to the notion that the text is fragile and needs protection from our demands or desires is to suggest that God's children are permitted less freedom, even illusory freedom, with their transitional object than any loving mother would allow her children with theirs. Despite their claims for the depths of God's parental love, preachers frequently find themselves nagged by doubts about their capacity to give life to a text that is more readily perceived as offering life to them.

At the end of these first few hours and days alone with the text I find scribbled on the yellow pad often foolish, sometimes brazen, frequently shameful, but usually honest and heartfelt questions and comments concerning the biblical passage— thoughts and insights that I now sense are genuinely my own. Whether by this time I have begun to make friends with the text or have instead become its enemy, we typically share a mutual respect and a common ground. The text and I have begun to establish our own relationship and to know where the other stands before inviting others to join and potentially diffuse the intensity of our conversation or play. We have done what we can to prevent others from determining our relationship for us. Whatever the text and I myself may ultimately reveal in the coming days of preparing for and preaching the sermon, that revelation now stands a better chance of being a collaborative word, a shared illusion, a truth both created and found.

The Capacity to Be Alone

Ministers or seminarians fortunate to have had a good-enough holding environment in childhood nonetheless must come to grips with unrelenting pressure to comply and to act with a pastoral demeanor prescribed by social custom. Churches and seminaries frequently overlook the unique beliefs, histories, or needs of their ministers or students or, conversely, focus overmuch on their personal idiosyncracies, discouraging the possibility of their simply playing alone with text and doctrine in order to discover what may spontaneously arise amid the benign but attentive presence of God and church.

Despite Winnicott's conviction that a healthy self emerges only from a good-enough primary relationship, he ultimately conceived of the self as quite solitary and needing to resist those excessive demands for conformity to the external environment so familiar to ministers. Just as the achievement of a secure silence between patient and therapist became for Winnicott the most promising sign of progress in psychotherapy, so too he nearly equated what he called an individual's capacity to be alone with emotional maturity.[15] Jay R. Greenberg and Stephen A. Mitchell point out that almost all Winnicott's contributions center around "the continually hazardous struggle of the self for an individuated existence which at the same time allows for intimate contact with others."[16]

For Winnicott, however, solitude is not the same as separation or isolation; one may be completely alone, as, for example, a prisoner in solitary confinement, without enjoying solitude. Solitude is not "a defiant declaration of one's capacity to go it alone."[17] To the contrary, Winnicott finds the origins of the capacity to be alone in a deeply relational experience "*of being alone, as an infant and small child, in the presence of mother.* Thus the basis of the capacity to be alone is a paradox; it is the experience of being alone while someone else is present."[18]

The caretaker who initially adapts to the needs of the infant, who in turn acknowledges the value of the infant's transitional object and who eventually oversees without undue interference the infant's solitary play, establishes a benign environment where the child can experience a state of formless quiescence, a kind of floundering or even inchoate boredom, from which some spontaneous gesture or desire (as for the spatula) may arise: "It is only when alone (that is to say, in the presence of someone) that the infant can discover his own personal life. The pathological alternative is a false life built on reactions to external stimuli."[19]

Being alone in the presence of another permits the discovery of authentic impulses and desires that belong solely to the infant. The accumulation of such experiences contributes to a sense that life is vitally *real* rather than hopelessly futile. What initially seems little more than an archaic precursor to boredom thus constitutes for Winnicott the child's source of authentic hope. Phillips explains:

> In ordinary states of boredom the child returns to the possibility of his own desire. That boredom is actually a precarious process in which the child is, as it were, both waiting for something and looking for something, in which hope is being secretly negotiated…In the muffled, sometimes irritable confusion of boredom the child is reaching to a recurrent sense of emptiness out of which his real desire can crystallize. But to begin with, of course, the child needs the adult to hold, and hold to, the experience—that is, to recognize it as such, rather than to sabotage it by distraction. The child's boredom starts as a regular crisis in the child's capacity to be alone in the presence of the mother. In other words, the capacity to be bored can be a developmental achievement for the child.[20]

Caretakers err in rushing to alleviate rather than simply acknowledging a child's boredom; a "premature flight from uncertainty" circumvents the negotiation of hope and condemns the child to a life that "must be, or be seen to be, endlessly interesting."[21]

One ironic consequence of impeding a child's or even one's own boredom is the rise of a compliant self discernible in part for its being boring—a false self whose primary tasks involve anticipating the needs of its external environment, caring for its caretakers, and minimizing any possibility of being surprised from within or without. Precocious concern for the needs of others deadens vitality by displacing the child's awareness of his or her own personal desires. The compliant child typically learns to elevate mind over body, curbing those harbingers of surprise of feeling or spirit by means of cognition and intellectualization. In Winnicott's words, "[T]he center of gravity of consciousness transfers from the kernel to the shell, from the individual to the care, the technique."[22]

In reflecting on the psychodynamics that compel a person to become boring, Masud Khan writes:

> One can see how clearly tiring and boring are related together, as techniques of coping with inner stress. The boring patient is trying to maintain omnipotent control over his inner reality by obsessional over-control of language and material. His narrative is petrified where nothing can happen…The patient who compels boring narrative on us is not letting language and metaphor elaborate or change his experience. He creates a space of discourse where both he and the analyst are paralysed by the technique of the narrative as well as its monotonous and repetitive contents…From this I would conclude that that which is boring is inherently inauthentic, both for the patient and the analyst. And yet we have to learn to tolerate this counterfeit discourse in order to help the patient.[23]

Compliant persons exhaust themselves and bore others by striving overmuch to screen their passions, to camouflage their impulses, to monitor their every word or motive, or to suppress anything surprising or unexpected. Shunning the risks of solitude or of actual boredom because of the uncertainties these evoke, they sacrifice kernel for shell, internal core for external care, spontaneous play for studied technique. "It is therefore another interesting paradox," comments Adam Phillips, "to note how much, for Winnicott, development depended on the capacity to relinquish or suspend concern for the object...[C]oncern for [another] is easily a compliant act and always potentially an obstacle to passionate intimacy and personal development."[24]

Why Are Ministers Compliant?

If ministry is nearly synonymous with extensive concern for others, pastors are especially vulnerable to compliance and therefore, according to Winnicott's formula, to becoming boring. The prosaic sermon, often justly thought to reflect the preacher's *lack* of preparation or concern for the congregation, could in this light as likely signify the preacher's *excessive* preparation or concern. To bore one's hearers could mean, oddly, to care too much for them.

The preacher is no doubt much to blame for this tangled state of affairs. Winnicott's observations, however, suggest a need for spreading responsibility more liberally. A young child develops precocious concern for others at the expense of personal vitality in response to an environment experienced as neglectful or overbearing. The compliant child either is forced to be prematurely alone or is instead never permitted to be alone, rather than more optimally allowed to be alone in the presence of another. So, too, preachers often experience their surroundings as alternately indifferent or overwhelming and feel subtly pressured to increase their compliance at the cost of diminishing self-awareness and vigor.

James Dittes speculated in the early 1970s that the origins of what he considered the personal and pastoral inhibitions or "cool bondage" of many ministers could be traced to their exaggerated desires as children to feel "assured of being on the same side as [their] parents by internalizing [their parents'] standards and enforcing them, on [themselves] and on others." He suggested that "it is entirely possible that in dealing with ministers we are often dealing with persons who *are* particularly dependent on such sources of support and well-being as parents represent, who are particularly likely to adopt such strategies to guarantee their support, and indeed who may have been particularly well practiced in just this process."[25]

More recently, Donald Capps has argued that the idiosyncratic but influential religious perspectives of William James, Rudolph Otto, Carl Jung, and Erik Erikson—all prominent figures in the twentieth-century psychology of religion—derived for each man from personal struggles with melancholia or chronic depression that "may be traced, ultimately, to the author's relationship with his own mother. The sadness, despair, and rage characteristic of melancholy have an object, and in these four cases this object is the author's mother." Capps continues, "It becomes their task to try to understand how religion serves as a stand-in for the mother, or for the son's relationship to his mother, and how, within his mature views on religion, there is a 'pre-historic core' that has to do with this relationship."[26]

Such observations continue to resonate in my own conversations primarily with seminary students, many of whom recall serving as a parentified child in their families of origin. They remember specific instances of what Winnicott would consider premature concern for others and recount, with deep shame or with notable pride, caring as children for needy, depressed, sexually overstimulating or otherwise exploitive parents or for lost or neglected siblings. They in turn have little difficulty understanding their present pursuit of ministry in terms of their familiar childhood roles and responsibilities.

Even apart from early family experiences, however, every seminary student or minister faces significant professional pressures to attend to the concerns of countless others, including not only the numerous and often legitimate pastoral needs of parishioners but, more subtly, to the beliefs and regulations of the "parent" church and its various pronouncements on one or another perplexing issues of the day. The church and its various constituencies, including seminaries, can sabotage ministers' boredom, circumvent their secret negotiation of hope, and condemn them to reactionary lives that must be, or seem to be, endlessly interesting.

The most public expression of all this, at least in those mainline churches most familiar to me, is the petrified and predictable sermon where nothing is allowed to happen. The preacher overly controls the language of the sermon, seeking to limit any surprising eruptions of emotion or spirit or any challenges to familiar patterns of belief or practice. Monotonous words and metaphors ringing of inauthenticity paralyze rather than elaborate or change human experience.

My intention here is to plead not for heresy in preaching, or for indifference to the gospel of Christ, or for a rejection of the institutional church, but more modestly for an increasing playfulness, honesty, confidence, and courage as preachers first approach a given biblical text. Because of our childhood proclivities to concern for others, however, and ongoing demands for such caring in our professional lives, we tend to *experience* the kind of authentic solitude that I am urging as an act of heresy, of indifference to Christ, or of betraying those on whose love we most depend. The stakes in such solitude with a text feel dangerously, precariously high.

Unless preacher and text alike first become vulnerable to the other while holding at bay outside authorities, including even God or Christ for a time, if such is even possible, there can be little hope that preacher or text will inspire anyone else. If the minister refuses to be changed by and, more provocatively, to "change" the text in this early encounter, the resulting sermon almost invariably will paralyze and bore rather than touch and transform. If play is akin to recreation, and recreation to re-creation, then Winnicott's vision for psychological health calls for a willingness to create and to be re-created again and again in relation to the beloved object. Playing alone with the text, finding and creating truth, is the first and foremost task, though not the last, in effective pastoral preaching.

Hearing the Word

We move now to consider a more tangible expression of one of my own such personal encounters with a lectionary text—the first of several sermons presented and then analyzed throughout the book. I delivered the following sermon as a baccalaureate address to seminary graduates, their families, friends, and teachers. The ceremony took place in late spring in the week prior to the church's commemoration of the ascension of the Lord. I titled the sermon "Downward Mobility."

■ ■ ■ ■

When [the apostles] had come together, they asked [the risen Christ], "Lord, is this the time when you will restore the kingdom to Israel?" He replied, "It is not for you to know the times or periods that the Father has set by his own authority. But you will receive power when the Holy Spirit has come upon you; and you will be my witnesses in Jerusalem, in all Judea and Samaria, and to the ends of the earth." When [Jesus] had said this, as they were watching, he was lifted up, and a cloud took him out of their sight. While he was going and they were gazing up toward heaven, suddenly two men in white robes stood by them. They said, "Men of Galilee, why do you stand looking up toward heaven? This Jesus, who has been taken up from you into heaven, will come in the same way as you saw him go into heaven."

Then they returned to Jerusalem from the mount called Olivet, which is near Jerusalem, a sabbath day's journey away. (Acts 1:6–12)

■ Downward Mobility ■

As suburban children we floated at night in swimming pools the temperature of blood; pools the color of Earth as seen from outer space. We would skinny-dip, my friends and me—hip-chick Stacey with her long yellow hair and Malibu Barbie body; Mark, our silent strongman; Kristy, our omni-freckled redheaded joke machine; voice-of-reason Julie, with her "statistically average" body; honey-bronze ski bum Dana, with his nonexistent tan line and suspiciously large amounts of cash; and Todd, the prude, always the last to strip, even then peeling off his underwear underneath the water. We would float and be naked—pretending to be embryos, pretending to be fetuses—all of us silent save for the hum of the pool filter. Our minds would be blank and our eyes closed as we floated in warm waters, the distinction between our bodies and brains reduced to nothing—bathed in chlorine and lit by pure blue lights installed underneath diving boards.[27]

So writes Douglas Coupland, unofficial spokesperson for Generation X, in his novel *Life After God.* Coupland says,

> Ours was a life lived in paradise and thus it rendered any discussion of transcendental ideas pointless. Politics, we supposed, existed elsewhere in a televised nonparadise; death was something similar to recycling. Life was charmed but without politics or religion. It was the life of the children of children of the pioneers—life after God—a life of earthly salvation on the edge of heaven…I think there was a trade-off somewhere along the line. I think the price we paid for our golden life was an inability to fully believe in love; instead we gained an irony that scorched everything it touched. And I wonder if this irony is the price we paid for the loss of God.[28]

Then Coupland adds:

> Some facts about me: I think I am a broken person…Sometimes I look back on my life and am surprised at the lack of kind things I have done. Sometimes I just feel that there must be another road that can be walked…Now—here is my secret: I tell it to you with the openness of heart that I doubt I shall ever achieve again, so I pray that you are in a quiet room as you hear these words. My secret is that I need God—that I am sick and can no longer make it alone. I need God to help me give, because I no longer seem to be capable of giving; to help me be kind, as I no longer seem capable of kindness; to help me love, as I seem beyond being able to love.[29]

■

> *[A]s they were watching, [Jesus] was lifted up, and a cloud took him out of their sight. While he was going and they were gazing up toward heaven, suddenly two men in white robes stood by them. They said, "Men of Galilee, why do you stand looking up toward heaven?"*

A strange question, really, given all they'd been through. Who *wouldn't* be gazing up there?

The risen Jesus ties up a few loose ends for his disciples, sets them straight one last time, says they shouldn't get all caught up with when they're going to come into their kingdom, that the life he has in mind for them isn't going to be just another entry in their PalmPilots® or Day-Timers®. *"It is not for you to know the times or periods that the Father has set by his own authority."* Not for them to know, they who knew plenty else after three years of training with the master. But they weren't going to know it all; there were some things for them not to know. Then he jets up into the clouds to vanish before their eyes, clouds that on most days still tend to keep him out of our sight. A couple of angelic types turn up here at the end just as they had with the shepherds at the beginning, just as with the women at the tomb, only to ask Jesus' still astonished followers, *"Why do you stand looking up toward heaven?"*

Well, why not? Why shouldn't they be gazing there? You can't really blame them for lingering there, straining to see something beyond the clouds. They had to have sensed that their foundations were shifting, that things were going to be different now when they journeyed back down the mountain, that their lives were about to change yet again. I think I'd hang around there some, too; I'd be gazing up toward heaven, too, if I were they.

What they couldn't have known back then but what you and I know all too well now is that we're still gazing there, still looking up as we're counting down to two thousand years later, straining in this life after God to see some face through the clouds, longing to feel some assurance that we're not alone, that things at last are going to be all right. But those clouds take him out of our sight.

■

It had been quite a day, full of anxiety, a familiar enough companion of mine even on more ordinary days than this. I had flown all the way across the country, carrying under my arms too many bags full of my life's possessions. I was twenty-two years old, heading from a summer internship in a Seattle church out to New Jersey to begin my seminary studies. I'd never been to New Jersey before, had never seen my new school, and to get there I took a train from Newark's Penn Station to Princeton Junction.

The loudspeakers on that train announcing the various stops were manufactured, I'm now convinced, by the same company that expanded into drive-through menus for fast-food restaurants; I couldn't understand a word that they were saying. Every time another stop was announced—Rahway, Metro Park, Metuchin, New Brunswick—for all I knew, the conductor could well have been asking, "Do you want fries with that?" or whatever those drive-through menus say. So every time a stop was announced, I'd get out of my seat, find a trainman, and ask if it had been Princeton that was called. I was worried, for I'd heard stories about the East. The conductor finally tired of my asking and assured me that he would personally come to find me before we stopped at Princeton Junction.

I got off the train with my life's possessions, found a taxi that delivered me right to my new dormitory doorstep, got the key to my room, put down my hundred pounds of baggage, closed the door, sat on the bare, green plastic mattress—exhausted, grateful to have survived, but wondering what on earth I was doing in this strange place where I knew not a soul. If anyone had asked in a less vulnerable moment, I probably would have answered that what I was doing there was coming to be a minister in service to Christ. But at that moment on my plastic mattress it was not quite so clear. A cloud had taken him out of my sight.

■

"Why are there so many songs about rainbows, and what's on the other side?" sings Kermit the Frog in one of his more sublime moments, and anyone with a remnant of soul knows the answer to his question. Douglas Coupland's secret is our secret, too, we who falter with him through this life after God— the secret that we need God, that we are broken persons, that we are sick and can no longer make it alone, that we need God to help us give, because we no longer seem capable of giving, to help us be kind, as we no longer seem capable of kindness, that we are loveless and seem beyond the ability to love. That's why there are so many songs about rainbows, Kermit, that's why we stand looking up toward heaven—hoping someone is there, needing someone to be there.

■

A few summers ago I traveled with a little group through Brazil, a land of striking contrast between opulence and poverty, a distinction increasingly mimicked by our own culture. On one day in particular a priest in the African-Brazilian coastal city of Salvador led us down to a little community, a shanty town, really, a *favela,* of the very poor. In desperation the people there had poured into the city from the barren countryside and squatted on a piece of government land on the shores of a bay. We walked through some of their little one-room shacks built on stilts over the water since there was no space left on land. You could see the water of the bay below through a small hole in the wood floor which served as the toilet. The air reeked of the raw sewage filling the bay.

As we walked from home to home, past the makeshift dirt soccer field, through a tiny stucco Catholic school, always surrounded by throngs of children who loved the priest, our guide, and who seemed delighted to have us there, I began to choke back tears. Tears amid such poverty should not have surprised me, but these tears did, because even at the time I knew that they were tears not of sadness but of joy, of envy, of longing even. It's hard to explain this without romanticizing poverty and destitution, which we must never do, but I knew as we walked that these people possessed something that I in my charmed paradise with swimming pools the temperature of blood, that we in our life after God, did not possess. I can't be certain, but I think my joy that day was a fleeting crack in the crust of irony that covers everything I touch, a tiny fissure in the sclerosis of secularism we suffer, we children of children of the pioneers who no longer fully believe in love—a momentary parting of the clouds through which I glimpsed in their faces the face of the one we are longing to see. I felt something there, enough to move me to tears if I hadn't contained them so well, a spirit of joy amid the stench, some longing in me not to give but to get something I sensed they had.

While he was going and they were gazing up toward heaven, suddenly two men in white robes stood by them. They said, "...Why do you stand looking up toward heaven?"

The angelic question seems a bit harsh to us who, with the disciples, are suckers for songs about rainbows and what's on the other side. For we're still gazing upward, you and I, looking for that face in the clouds, hoping that Jesus will high-tail it back here before our computers crash for want of his coming. Can't the angels see that, couldn't they be a bit more understanding, a little more sympathetic?

But more and more I'm beginning to wonder if the angels aren't right—that the face we're looking for, you and I, is far more likely to be found, on those rare occasions when it's glimpsed at all, not in the clouds of spiritual heights but far down the mountain in the stench of soulful depths, in a ministry of downward mobility, in embarrassingly modest tasks of witness and prayer. There's nothing wrong with spiritual heights, of course, and with Kermit and with Jesus' disciples I imagine we'll be singing songs about rainbows, searching for his face through the clouds, until Jesus really does come thus again. But the angels' reproach urging us to look for him in the depths and not the heights makes more and more sense to me, maybe to you too.

■

I sat on my green plastic mattress in that new dormitory room staring at nothing for some time and was startled out of my cloudy fog by a knock at the door. I opened it to find standing there Dr. David Dilworth, the kindly pastor of the Seattle internship church from whence I had just come, and one person about as close to the likes of Jesus as anyone I've known, but on that day outdoing even himself. I was stunned. I couldn't believe my eyes. The first person to greet me in my new home across the country the same man I'd left just a little before!

He'd had a meeting in Princeton that day, he said, and just wanted to stop by to see if I'd made it and all. I told him how empty I'd felt, wondering what I was doing there, and how glad I was to see his face. After what couldn't have been more than a few minutes or so he asked if he might pray for me to get this whole seminary show rolling. We prayed, he left, and I wept. A simple act of ministry for him, a glimpse of Christ's face in the lonely depths for me.

■

Why are there so many songs about rainbows, why do we stand looking up toward heaven, when Jesus has so much *less* in store for us down here? You're more likely to see him when you're looking down, not up, say those angels—looking at the poor, looking anxious and alone, looking at the broken children of children of the pioneers in this scorched and loveless paradise after God.

"You will receive power when the Holy Spirit has come upon you; and you will be my witnesses in Jerusalem, in all Judea and Samaria, and to the ends of the earth."

Jesus says to them there at the end, here at the end: Dear friends, dear little disciples of Jesus Christ, it's time to go down the mountain. But not to worry, you will receive power, Jesus says. You will be my witnesses. You will. You will.

Responding to the Word

As noted, this sermon was preached just prior to Ascension Sunday at a baccalaureate service for graduating seminarians. In this case one direct link between the special occasion of the sermon and the lectionary text became immediately apparent, namely, that graduating seminarians, not unlike Jesus' disciples in the aftermath of his ascension, suddenly face an uncertain future. The sermon centers on taking courage and forgoing certainties, and in this respect lifts up the very traits that I am advocating for preachers in their initial encounters with a biblical text.

Playing with the Text

In looking back over various comments that I jotted on a yellow pad in preparing this sermon—pages I usually retain and later file with the final sermon manuscript—what surfaces is my initial impatience with the disciples and the angels but also, to a lesser degree, with Jesus in this text. I noted that the disciples still seemed to expect a quick political fix from Jesus ("Lord, is this the time...?") and that he responded by telling them—even after their three years together, a period of similar length to seminary training—that they simply were not to know. I wondered whether there was any contradiction between his asking them to bear witness to him and his preventing them from knowing all that they wanted to know about him. "Will they know enough to be able to bear witness?" I asked—a question frequently posed by graduating seminary students and their teachers as well. I also asked, more mundanely, "What exactly is a sabbath day's journey?"

The angels, too, I wrote, "give a confusingly mixed message" here. On the one hand, they appear to reproach the disciples for straining to see Jesus beyond the clouds, but, on the other hand, seem to legitimize their upward gaze by suggesting that Jesus will return in the very same manner. I noted, too, that angels seem to arrive only at pivotal moments in Jesus' life—his birth, his resurrection, here his ascension—and wondered what to make of this.

Equally evident to me in these early notes, in retrospect, is a weariness more personal than theological. "Why couldn't Jesus stick around longer, and why is he so slow to return, if he's coming at all?" I wrote, a theologically legitimate if obvious question but, given the comments that followed, one more likely reflecting my own feelings at the end of an academic year. These comments include, "My exhaustion—the seminary as a total [meaning 'all-consuming'] institution," followed by references to several specific institutional battles recently waged. "We accuse each other of looking down, away from God, or looking inward, narcissistic, selfish," I told myself, and added more grimly, "Think of this as a funeral sermon for the outgoing class—your death, your conclusion, your last rites."

Amid these somewhat petulant comments, however, were more positive thoughts as well. I noted that "looking up" may be a kind of prayer and "looking down" a kind of witnessing, together comprising the significant postures of the spiritual life and linked geographically in the text to Mount Olivet and to Jerusalem, respectively. I scribbled a number of memories of times in my life of yearning to see God more clearly and recalled moments when I feared being left alone. Although unusual in my experience in this earliest stage of preparation, in this particular case several of the stories and connections that eventually found their way into the actual sermon—the shanty town of Brazil, the memories of my first day at seminary, and Kermit the Frog's song about rainbows, along with several other stories that I did not ultimately use—occurred to me in these initial sessions alone with the text. However, the Coupland material from *Life After God*—which I explore further in the following chapter on the role of stories from contemporary life—came to mind only later in the sermon preparation process.

In these early readings my eyes almost hypnotically kept returning to the angels' question, "Men of Galilee, why do you stand looking up toward heaven?" Were I to approach this same text at another time or under different circumstances, another aspect of the narrative would likely capture my attention. In preparing this sermon, however, the angels' question kept pressing itself on me and, as I attempt to show in the final sections of this analysis, eventually came to ease my weariness; text and preacher managed to find common ground and mutual regard.

Nuts and Bolts

We have been considering in this chapter some dynamics of the earliest stage of sermon preparation involving the preacher's initial personal encounter with a biblical text. Even at this early stage, however, it is possible to anticipate ways in which this first encounter may become manifest in the final drafting and delivery of the sermon.

Because those who hear sermons, myself included, often have difficulty remembering the specific words or even the general thrust of the biblical text after hearing it read only once, I generally repeat a particular line from the biblical text several times in the sermon. This repetition usually occurs at transitional points linking sections that exposit scripture to those that recount contemporary stories or that make explicit theological claims. In hearing the central scriptural theme or a unifying theological thread throughout the sermon, the listener intuits that a transition is taking place. This approach eliminates need for wordy transitional markers such as, for example, "In our scripture lesson today we notice that…," or "This passage reminds me of the time when I first traveled to seminary," or similar formulaic expressions.

In the present sermon, of course, the angels' question that commanded my attention in early readings of the text, "Why do you stand looking up toward heaven?" and the words, "A cloud had taken him out of their sight," serve as the primary transitional expressions and are here at times playfully reinforced by Kermit the Frog's related question, "Why are there so many songs about rainbows?" In nearly every transition of this sermon some variation of at least one of these three phrases may be found. As the sermon draws to its conclusion, these transitional strands come together into more enduring relationship.

My hope is that frequent repetition will cause the listener to come away from the sermon remembering, word-for-word, at least one important line from the biblical text. I also desire, however, that this key theme will be remembered in the broader context of the entire lectionary passage. To this end I attempt to work a significant portion of the original biblical text into the body of the sermon as seamlessly as possible, but additionally seek to retell the essential details of the biblical narrative in contemporary idiom, optimally without trivializing or demeaning the text.

In the present sermon this exposition begins in mid-text immediately after the angels' question has been first introduced, by initially focusing on the thematic thread ("A strange question, really, given all they'd been through") but then quickly retracing my steps back to the beginning of the passage. Here, in saying that "the risen Jesus ties up a few loose ends," or that "they shouldn't get all caught up," or that "he jets up into the clouds to vanish before their eyes," I try to enliven the text while striving to avoid cynicism or dramatic excess. In the space of just one paragraph this rehearsal of the biblical text comes full circle to again tack down the focal question of the angels, leading in turn to a brief, two-paragraph foray into more existential claims of the sermon ("that their foundations were shifting, that things were going to be different now," or "What they couldn't have known back then but what you and I know all too well now is that we're still gazing there").

Most readers will have noticed in this sermon that I chose not to raise critical textual and historical questions concerning whether Jesus really ascended bodily into heaven, or what "up" actually means given a contemporary cosmology, or whether the author of Luke–Acts intended a thematic link between this passage and the earlier account of Jesus' transfiguration in Luke 9, or whether angels truly appeared to the disciples on a mountain. I personally wrestle with such questions in my study of the Bible and occasionally allow them to surface as a specific emphasis in a sermon. Typically, however, I subjugate them to the text's more pressing existential or theological claims.

I find an unlikely ally for this choice of emphasis in Winnicott's convictions concerning the psychological necessity of shared illusory phenomena, as well as in postmodern philosophical conventions that could otherwise be construed to relativize or decimate particular faith claims. In his book *The Word as True Myth,* for example, Gary Dorrien writes:

> The postmodern critique of Enlightenment foundationalism and universalism opens a space for religious discourse that modern rationalism excluded...If all knowledge is socially constructed, partial, and open to unending interpretation, theological claims are hardly disadvantaged by their mythical character. Many academic disciplines today are only beginning to acknowledge that their knowledge is constructed and perspectival. The fact that theologians have struggled for the past two centuries to deal with the relativity of their discipline makes theology better prepared than some disciplines to function in a postmodern environment.[30]

Dorrien seems to confirm what Winnicott would describe as the inherent integrity of the potential or transitional space between objective and subjective realities; he argues in effect that in having for so long fallen so far behind in the Enlightenment's race for falsifiable truth, theology in a post-Enlightenment age suddenly appears to be far ahead of the pack. Even "hard" sciences today confront the relativity of their unique claims to reality, locating their truths in a space somewhere between pure fact and invented fiction. Theology, in having struggled with this relativity for two centuries, may now be uniquely equipped among the disciplines to guide the way.

Postmodern conventions may be reflecting or contributing as well to changes in the ways that people listen to sermons. For those listeners, and perhaps especially young listeners, increasingly accustomed to postmodern ways of thinking, the preacher no longer need dwell so extensively on the cosmology of ascension or on questions of the existence of angels, and can make room instead for a shared realm of necessary illusion.

Text and Transformation

For the many obvious differences in social setting and communication style that distinguish pastoral counseling and pastoral preaching, I have become more and more convinced that people listen to sermons for much the same reason that they seek out pastoral counseling, namely, out of a deep and usually unspoken desire that their present lives be somehow transformed. Although some ministers may feel uneasy in making such a claim, the purpose of preaching, to my mind like that of counseling, is somehow simply to change people or, at least, to enhance their potential for change.

As Winnicott demonstrated in the spatula game and elsewhere, however, children and adults alike fiercely resist any change perceived as being coerced or compelled by another. Yet they embrace change felt to be freely invited by a good-enough holding environment. People change, that is to say, when they experience sufficient safety and freedom to change.[31] Theories of preaching, then, like theories of psychotherapy, become guides to the intricate art of establishing the safety necessary to enable faithful transformation and change.

Establishing this secure environment for change in preaching involves in part allowing the listening congregation to meet the biblical text in much the same way that the preacher first encountered it days or even weeks earlier. Biblical truth for the congregation, just as for the preacher, must be at once both created and found. In the present sermon I attempt to establish this safety by initially siding with the apostles over against the angels ("A strange question, really, given all they'd been through," and "Well, why not? Why shouldn't they be gazing there?"), even as in my own early readings I experienced the angels' question more as a reproach than as an invitation. I take the risk of assuming here that those who hear the narrative for the first time may identify, as I did, with the apostles' desire to keep searching the heavens for their suddenly absent Lord and friend. I hope to meet the listeners at a comfortable place and to remain there with them for a considerable period of time, since as preacher I am no longer merely the child playing alone with the text but now also the mother or therapist inviting the congregation's own solitary play. In this sense preaching becomes less one's leading a congregation to some predetermined place than creating a benign space for finding its own interests and desires.

In returning a second time to the biblical passage much later in the sermon, I begin where I had previously left off by again identifying with the apostles ("The angelic question seems a bit harsh to us who, with the disciples, are suckers for songs about rainbows..."). This time, however, I am trusting that the earlier stories about my loneliness in arriving at seminary and my surprising joy amid Brazilian poverty, as well as the sheer winsomeness of Kermit the Frog as star-gazing companion, have served to soften resistance to an alternate reading of the angels' question in the text. Having heard acknowledged that the angels' question seems somewhat harsh and that the preacher and listeners alike long to see Jesus' face, the congregation may be better able to hear, as I myself eventually was, encouragement rather than chastisement in the biblical text's question, as if the angels are in essence saying, "You won't find Jesus here, but we *can* suggest where you may be able to find him." The congregation may now be more ready to tolerate the angels' attempt, it seems, to direct the apostles to seek out Jesus in places where they previously may not have wanted to go.

Still, I seek not simply to dismiss the hearers' or my own prior understanding of the text as foolish or inadequate ("There's nothing wrong with spiritual heights, of course"). Even the text and the angels, in my view, allow for this leniency in their saying, for example, that "this Jesus...will come in the same way as you saw him go." At this point, however, we are newly willing to entertain that our chances of finding Jesus would actually be enhanced by expanding our search to include increasingly threatening venues ("Not in the clouds of spiritual heights but far down the mountain in the stench of soulful depths"). Here the sermon's stories and scripture carry the full weight of this new understanding, enticing listeners to freely change without the preacher's having to resort to coercion, shaming, or moralizing. The happy ending to my story of loneliness in coming to seminary reinforces the message that Jesus *is* sometimes found far down the mountain, and the sermon's closing words echo the biblical text's promise that Jesus will remain close at hand even there.

CHAPTER 2

Playing Witness to Life

Earl Palmer, the pastor of a church where I interned briefly while in college, gave me some advice that he himself had received years earlier from George Buttrick, then pastor of the Madison Avenue Presbyterian Church in New York City. Speaking at a senior breakfast at Princeton Theological Seminary to the need for ministers to read beyond what their parishioners were reading, Buttrick told Palmer's graduating class, "If you're telling your people about Coney Island, don't tell them only about the amusements and concession stands that everyone can see; tell them about the mysteries of the sea that no one sees."

I have remembered these words in the intervening years, especially after having moved to Princeton, New Jersey, to attend seminary, when I would sometimes drive past Coney Island, just an hour or so away on my way to JFK airport. What, as preacher, would I read? What would I tell the people? What mysteries would I discover that others might not notice regarding whatever the subject at hand?

If ministers are to avoid expositing the obvious, they must be able to see something—some subtlety, some singularity, some mystery—that others overlook. Interest in sermons is generated, I have argued, less from any exaggerated rhetorical attempt on the part of the preacher to be amusing, provocative, or, for that matter, even interesting, than from a much more private and preverbal or even infantile encounter with a biblical text in an environment that minimizes pressures for social and doctrinaire compliance. When these familiar constraints and inhibitions are lifted, ministers are often surprised, but sometimes troubled, to discover memories, thoughts, appetites, and desires beginning to surface from previously uncharted depths; they find themselves venturing beyond the amusements and concession stands and confronting the mysteries of the sea.

The present chapter seeks to guide ministers in recognizing and accepting their own unique and sometimes unsavory interests and desires while attempting to fathom particular mysteries and in practicing what one of my own mentors in preaching often called the "exegesis of life."[1] It continues to build on psychoanalytic theory in general and on Winnicott's legacy in particular, by drawing on essays by Adam Phillips on the nature of curiosity. I seek to show here that in the minister's capacity to *play* witness to what may be God's subtle workings of love amid unremarkable or extreme settings of life, and then to *bear* witness to these intimations of grace, the boundaries between pastoral tasks of care and of proclamation become less distinctly drawn. Playing witness and bearing witness to life comprise our second key focus for vital pastoral preaching.

Preparing for the Word

In a meditation on Psalm 8 ("What are human beings that you are mindful of them?") written in the years immediately following his conversion to Christianity, Augustine found allegorically prefigured in its beasts of the field, birds of the air, and fish of the sea (of vv. 7–8) the sins of sensual pleasure, human arrogance, and insatiable interest. He writes, "These three kinds of vices, that is, carnal pleasure (*voluptas carnis*), pride (*superbia*), and curiosity (*curiositas*), comprehend all sin."[2]

It is no small irony that Augustine, whose later *Confessions* launched a literary genre that would demonstrate the fecundity of his own compelling curiosity, counts curiosity among the most deadly of sins. The same curiosity that several years earlier had taunted the young man Augustine to "take...and read" the biblical words that would seal his own conversion and that just a few years thereafter would inspire him to reflect on the means whereby he had come to faith is implicated in his reflection on the psalm as a root of all sinfulness.[3] Such a condemnation of curiosity by a forebear of modern Western introspection reflects how longstanding is Christian theology's ambivalent attitude toward curiosity, a tendency perhaps even predated in the garden of Eden by the first couple's curiosity concerning the knowledge of good and evil but lingering today in the distrust of their desires by many contemporary ministers and others of faith. If God, as Augustine asserts in his reading of the psalm, has indeed elevated humanity to a status of dominion over its sensuality, pride, and curiosity, it seems at least worth questioning whether by such dominion God intended their complete annihilation.

Presumably Augustine himself and theologians who followed sought to retain certain desires and curiosities in the Christian repertoire—those "hungers of the heart"[4] of Augustine's own restless pursuit after God. If, however, allowances are to be made for *some* curiosities, how then can one go about distinguishing acceptable interests and appetites from those that are not? Furthermore, what may be revealed or concealed by the choices— by the diagnostic classifications—that one makes in this regard? More to the point, is it acceptable for Christians to be curious, at least, about curiosity?

Curiosity Disorders

"Psychoanalysis," writes Adam Phillips, is "about what killed people's appetite, about how we are most intimidated by the only thing that can sustain us. So it was to the fate of interest—of that imaginative hunger called curiosity, which is part of what I'm calling the love of life—in each person's life that Freud turned his attention. Having things to look forward to, making things to look forward to, he realized, can become a lost art."[5] Psychoanalysis, Phillips argues, is primarily a treatment for curiosity disorders, for a breakdown in people's capacity to find or make interests. It pursues whatever may have killed a person's appetite for life, what destroyed someone's sense "that the world is a promising place to live in," or what diminished one's relationship to hope. "People come for psychoanalysis when they are feeling undernourished," Phillips suggests, and, in this light, psychological diagnoses become then descriptions of various ways people starve themselves or have been starved of their interests or ideals.[6]

Although to some degree inevitable, this lack or loss of appetite for life is not inborn, but learned. Children, Phillips points out, tend to be experts in what interests them, and he recasts what Winnicott more ominously termed a necessary infantile "omnipotence" (over the mother, the breast, or the transitional object) as rather simply a child's "ecstacy of opportunity," that is, a child's ability to be "deranged by hope and anticipation—by ice cream," or even more succinctly as a child's "passionate love of life." For the child, Phillips writes, "'Meaning' is the polite word, the sophisticated word for pleasure."[7]

Children are naturally, gleefully, and for adults sometimes frustratingly curious, and part of Freud's original and continuing contribution was to notice that children's curiosities are centered, more often than not, in pleasures and mysteries of the human body—in what goes into and comes out of them and in the considerable sensual pleasures that they conjure and excite—or in what Freud provocatively called infantile sexuality. Phillips writes:

> In "'Civilized' Sexual Morality and Modern Nervous Illness" Freud makes a simple and still astonishing assertion: "the sexual behaviour of a human being often lays down the pattern for all his other modes of reacting to life." Integral to, indeed constitutive of, the sexual behavior of children is their curiosity about sex. One could almost say that their curiosity *is* their sexuality.[8]

These early interests in the human body, Freud realized, must eventually and inevitably be tamed by education and other functions of "civilized" culture through its various injunctions to sexual abstinence. This so-called civilized morality, however, comes with a high and usually hidden cost, evident in "an increase of anxiety about life and of fear of death" as well as in a preponderance of persons Freud referred to as "well-behaved weaklings who later become lost in the great mass of people that tend to follow, unwillingly, the leads given by strong individuals"—this latter conviction echoed in Winnicott's case against compliance and the tyranny of the false self.[9]

Thus, education and other expressions of civilized culture—including, of course, various forms of religion and even, Phillips presumes, psychoanalysis itself—become "forerunners of [what Freud would later call] the death instinct." It is, for Freud, "the function of culture to kill curiosity," or at least to distract people from their most basic curiosities by what he described in the same paper as "sublimation," a term derived from a process in chemistry whereby a solid (in psychoanalytic theory, the physical body and its sexual interests) is transformed into a vapor (here, into language, education, or spirituality). Children are hedonists, Freud argued, "preoccupied with the erotics of pleasure," but the task of civilization is to "foreclose the child's real interest" by offering various substitutes instead.[10] However, when abstinence or sublimations fail to take adequate account of the usually unconscious but still insistent interests of the sensual body, various symptoms often result. If these symptoms become sufficiently troublesome, they lead the suffering person into the care of recognized healers or priests of the culture.

This brings us to the horns of a dilemma, for in turning for relief to medicine, psychotherapy, education, or religion, the suffering person seeks strategies for transformation from those very agencies of culture that, according to psychoanalytic theory, created the problem in the first place. How can a representative of the culture aid in healing whatever loss of appetite for life, whatever curiosity disorder has been pressed upon the individual by that very culture? Of what use is Augustine's desire to curtail desire to one whose suffering stems from curtailed desire?

Passion Stories

One way to begin to engage, though never fully to resolve, this quandary may be to draw on subversive elements within these various cultural forms themselves. Jesus' teaching, for example, that one must become like a little child to enter the kingdom of God (Mt. 18:3) resonates with the similarly jarring psychoanalytic recognition that being a child entails interest in one's passions and curiosity about sex. In their efforts to elevate the status of children and children's passions, both Christian faith and psychoanalytic theory, while inevitably rooted in culture, nonetheless also run potentially crosscurrent to culture. In my desire, then, to begin to reclaim for pastoral preaching something of this unsettling but potentially therapeutic childlike curiosity and passion, despite their ambiguities, I offer two "passion" stories of my own.

A friend whose field is historical theology asked me what I had been working on recently, and I told him that I had been thinking about various ways ubiquitous electric light and the dearth of light from fire in the twentieth century may have contributed to a growing secularism or decreasing sense of the holy in contemporary life. He looked puzzled at first by this response but shortly became intrigued and even animated as a lively conversation ensued. As our exchange drew to a close, my friend impulsively remarked, "You know, it's not fair; you pastoral theologians can study whatever you damn well please." I smiled and agreed; our shared perception of the differences in the acceptable latitude of inquiry in our respective fields did not seem quite fair. His spontaneous comment, however, served to reinforce my conviction that, at some point long before or during their professional training, ministers and theologians typically learn to hesitate to pursue their own particular passions or to remain interested in what interests them.

Another passion story: After the baccalaureate service in which I had preached the sermon of the previous chapter, a man who identified himself as the father of one of the graduating seminarians came up to me and, referring to the story of the skinny-dipping youth, told me that I was right about how young people no longer had any moral standards these days. I nodded and mumbled something in response but lacked the courage to tell him that he had grossly misunderstood my intentions. Even if I had possessed such courage, it is unlikely he would have wanted to hear that far from deploring them, in many respects I *am* those youth and, in other respects, actually envied their values. Could I have told him that at least some part of me regretted not having shared in my youth their sexual freedom despite the costs, and that my having led the congregation to believe I was speaking autobiographically at the outset of the sermon may well have derived from this very regret? Would the man have wanted to hear that I told this story less to be provocative than because, in first coming across it myself, *I* was provoked by its eroticism and by the emotional aftertaste of its description of what seemed my own golden "life of earthly salvation on the edge of heaven"? Could I have said that, as little as I understood my own intentions in these matters, I chose this story less to speak of "kids these days" than of adults these days, institutions these days, churches these days, ministers these days, but especially myself these days? Or more simply that I chose this story just because it interested me?

What kills a minister's appetite? Is it, in part, the professional constraints, whether perceived or real, of various fields of theological inquiry, a fear of what the experts will think? Is it a fear that one risks being misunderstood from the pulpit as person or preacher or, perhaps worse, that one risks being exposed and thereby understood? What becomes of a preacher's childhood curiosity or love of life, of her ability to find and make interests? When does the world become less than a promising place for the preacher to live, and when does he become starved of desire or lose interest in human bodies? At what point do one's sublimations become so vaporous or spiritualized as to become symptomatic and depleting?

The Capacity to Waste Time

After having mulled over a biblical text for several hours or days, many ministers begin to feel mounting internal pressure to muster up some kind of story or lesson from life by which to "illustrate" what they now assume the text is saying. The minister seeks to draw from what seems an ever-dwindling supply of contemporary stories or personal experiences some examples of what the biblical writer (or some expert interpreter or traditional dogma) is believed to have understood about the life of faith. But this heightened anxiety and usual strategy for attempting to alleviate it tend prematurely to privilege, however subtly, other persons' interests and experiences of faith and life over those of the minister.

What might happen instead if at this still preliminary point in the process of sermon preparation, the minister, rather than concentrating on finding a story to illustrate what the text is presumed to be saying, were to focus intently on some particular concern or interest of her own regardless of its perceived relevance to the biblical text? What if the minister viewed this stage of the process simply as an oasis of much-needed personal time—an hour, two hours, or more—for intensive daydreaming about an unresolved problem in his life or family, or about an unsettling development in the neighborhood or abroad, or about a seemingly trite but interesting article in a recent newspaper?

Permitting themselves to daydream at length about whatever currently happens to be of some interest to them may strike many ministers as an extravagance they cannot afford, as a waste of their limited sermon preparation time. They may wonder, not without certain justification, what would happen if they were to spend hours contemplating something of personal interest that finally proved to have no bearing whatsoever on the sermon text. While coming up short in this way is indeed a risk one takes in the approach that I am advocating, even greater risks come into play when preachers too long neglect their own passions.

I have found in my own preaching that taking some hours of prime preparation time for reflection on a personal interest or concern has almost always borne fruit in the final outcome of the sermon. Engaging one's own curiosity and desire as preacher leads to an intimate involvement with the sermon seldom lost on the listening congregation. That the preacher attends at this point to passions of personal significance is far more important than that those passions promise to hold obvious relevance to a text or congregation.

In practicing this approach I have increasingly come to appreciate and trust the contagious nature of curiosity itself. If I myself am truly interested in the subject at hand, whatever it may be, I notice that other people usually grow interested themselves, if not necessarily in the specific issue or topic, then at least in the fact of my own interest in it. Just as my historical theologian friend became engaged by my interest in the relation of electric light to secularism, or as the father of the graduating seminarian found himself caught up by my interest in the skinny-dipping youth, so a congregation notices and finds contagious the preacher's personal investment in a sermon. In observing this contagion over time, preachers may begin to discover an increasing confidence or trust in following where their curiosity invites them to go. Preachers who, in seeking to listen to their lives, can resist for a time their ecclesial inheritance of ambivalence over curiosity may find themselves becoming again the little children "deranged by hope and anticipation—by ice cream" that they once knew themselves to be.

Pursuing the Mundane

To assist my students in this process, I sometimes ask someone in the class to volunteer something of interest, however ordinary, that has happened on that particular day. One student recently responded by saying that he was surprised by a black squirrel that caught his eye on campus that morning. Such a sighting, of course, would normally garner only a fleeting thought in that student's stream of consciousness. But what would happen, I proceed to wonder aloud with the class, if the student were to daydream about his interest in that squirrel for, say, a full fifteen minutes?

If the student is open to such a suggestion, the rest of the class and I begin asking him whatever questions come to mind. He might be asked, What was it about the particular squirrel that caught your eye? The student might then reveal that squirrels seem to him to be quite free, or that they seem excessively nervous and jumpy; he might admit that he didn't realize that there were such things as black squirrels, or that he was first startled by its color but then by the fact that he even noticed its color; he might suggest that he envies how easily squirrels seem to play, or offer that when he was a boy he once killed a squirrel with his BB gun, and so on—each of these responses potentially leading to further revelations.

If the student continues to be willing to tolerate the self-exposure that this little exercise inevitably entails, usually within a matter of minutes we find ourselves delving beneath the amusements and concession stands of black squirrels in the student's life to far more existentially penetrating and less comfortable mysteries of the sea (or better, in this case, mysteries of the "tree"). Although I interrupt the questioning before it reaches a point where the student might regret having revealed too much too soon to his classmates, it quickly becomes apparent that even a fleeting interest in a black squirrel may hold personal meanings not immediately apparent, yet accessible to those willing to pursue them just beneath the surface. I am increasingly convinced that the primary, perhaps the only, way to gain access to certain of these submerged meanings and passions may be via the often fleeting and arcane particularities—the black squirrels—of daily living.

If ministers were to regularly practice this discipline of tracking a specific interest or concern for a period of an entire hour—if, that is to say, they were to spend as much time and energy in sermon preparation attending to their "squirrel" of the day as to the lectionary text—would we not expect that, in addition to the shallows, they would increasingly engage the depths of their own lives and of life around them? Would we not expect them, over time, to discover more subtle movements of the Spirit, as well as ever-widening circles and sources of their own interests: personal thoughts, feelings, triumphs, and tragedies over the course of a day or a lifetime; books, magazines, newspapers, or even tabloids; comments from parishioners or from strangers at the supermarket; toys, hobbies, and recreational pursuits; or the intricate details of the worlds of politics, science, sports, religion, glamour, or congregational life? Would we not find preachers increasingly inclined to be intrigued once again by ice cream, by everyday life?

A manila file in my desk drawer is filled with assorted and sundry articles clipped from newspapers or magazines that, for reasons mostly unexplored, I once found alluring enough to put there. I remove one or another of the articles from time to time in preparing a sermon, usually without its having any obvious bearing on the lectionary text that I have already begun to study. On closer scrutiny, however, I almost always find that just beneath its surface lies some partial but gracious and personally significant truth with potential for wide application and broad appeal.

Some ministers may wonder whether by indulging in introspection over so ordinary an interest as a black squirrel or ice cream or a magazine article they demean the dignity of their divine calling. Would not the task of bearing witness to the majesty and mystery of a transcendent God be diminished by a preacher's mundane interests and passions? How much insight into God's overwhelming grace or justice, after all, can a squirrel finally reveal?

Not unlike Emerson's plea for preachers made of tuneable metal instead of malleable clay, James Dittes challenges ministers' concerns for contaminating the transcendent with particularity and their reticence for specificity and directness in preaching. A preacher's reluctance to be direct and particular, ostensibly out of deference to the transcendent, Dittes claims,

> is precisely what sabotages his loyalty to the transcendent. The absence of a vigorous style or of any style at all annuls his communication from the pulpit. So does his very inability to take a single idea and, leaving aside the many qualifications and the many companion ideas, to develop it vigorously and thoroughly. Because he cannot comfortably preach with particulars and in partialness, he cannot preach at all the important truths in whose name he abstains from partial and limited statement.[11]

Dittes's convictions concerning the particular and the partial in preaching reflect the embodied specificity of a little child's passions, which could lead to a culturally subversive but compelling and potentially healing kind of preaching.

Words Made Flesh

The primary instruments of healing in both psychotherapy and pastoral ministry are, significantly, words, and often words alone. Words serve as something of a mysterious intermediary between culture and self, coming into one's physical body from the culture but likewise going out from it back into the culture. As defining aspects of a culture, words and language inevitably contribute to problems related to cultural conformity; they also serve as the principal means by which we attempt to redress those very problems. Phillips contends that, not unlike preaching and pastoral care, psychoanalysis is "a rhetoric that persuades the patient that certain ways of describing his life will improve it," and that "whatever else it is, [psychoanalysis] is learning a language which, ideally, will make things better."[12]

More specifically, effective healing in both psychotherapy and pastoral preaching seems regularly to depend on words that speak especially to neglected sensual interests and desires of a person's physical body. While acquiring language is perhaps the primary means by which a child's attention begins to shift away from archaic sexual interests ("Language is the cure for infancy," Phillips observes), children's words nevertheless remain for them significantly embodied. Their words link newly realized verbal selves to the sensual pursuits of their preverbal selves—words as a "route back to bodies" in part expressing their curiosity about sex.[13] Thus, in psychotherapy and pastoral ministries alike, words of healing and transformation tend to be incarnate words— graphic, graspable, tangible words—somehow tied to the yearnings of the physical body.

Dismembered, spiritualized, or gnostic words—those that have somehow failed to emerge from the therapist's or preacher's own felt sense of longing or desire—will be incapable of untangling the costly attempts of others to turn their own passions into something acceptable. If the words of their respective professional canons do not engage the particular passions of therapists or preachers themselves, neither will they likely engage the passions of persons in their care. In choosing carefully their words of healing and transformation, psychotherapists, pastoral counselors, and preachers alike might themselves benefit from Freud's wistful advice for little boys: "If [they] could follow the hints given by the excitation of the penis they would get a little nearer to the solution of the problem."[14] (One early rejection by Christian theology of precisely this kind of hint, incidentally, may be found in the *Confessions,* where the mature Augustine recalls with disdain the pride taken by his father, Patricius, in his adolescent son's burgeoning manhood on witnessing his erection at the public baths.)[15]

How can those whose livelihood depends principally on words rejoin their words to bodies, to the passions of their preverbal depths? How can they overcome the difficulties that stem from having to use words to describe things unsuitable for words?[16]

Surviving Death

One tentative place to begin, returning again to Winnicott, may be in finding what words of their culture and canons will survive their own murderous rage. Phillips turns to a brief address that Winnicott delivered in 1950 to a group of psychology and social work students, entitled "Yes, But How Do We Know It's True?" Winnicott describes there two stages through which students typically pass in learning psychology, with parallels for students of divinity as well. "In the first stage," Winnicott writes,

> they learn what is being taught about psychology just as they learn the other [subjects]. In the second stage, they begin to wonder—yes, but is it true, is it real, how do we know? In the second stage, the psychological teaching begins to separate out from the other as something that can't just be learnt. It has to be felt as real, or else it is irritating and even maddening...Whereas most types of [learning] take you out of yourself, psychology, the psychology that matters, tends to throw you back into yourself...We can try to be objective and we can make every effort to learn about people without developing morbid introspection, but this requires effort, and you feel disturbed; this psychology is not going to behave itself properly as the other subjects in the curriculum do.[17]

For Winnicott, a student moves beyond the rote learning of compliance-based education to that point of truly engaging a discipline in much the same way that an infant gains a realistic perception of an object's separate existence, that is, by embodying or "chewing" on, and eventually "killing" it.

An object becomes "real," Winnicott claims, only by first surviving its own death. Although initially the child simply relates to an object as if it were part of the child's own self, eventually he or she seeks to destroy it. Only if the object can survive the child's hatred and its own destruction does it become fully real and loved by the child. Winnicott believed that this process repeated itself in adolescence, such that in growing to full maturity, healthy youth must eventually, in a sense, "kill" their parents—through testing, rebellion, moodiness, or ideological challenges—and yet optimally find their parents to have survived.[18] This sequence of object-relating to object-destroying to object-loving is, according to Winnicott, what leads to an awareness of distinctive boundaries between internal and external realities and to the possibility of truly loving relations with others. The object—the other or Other—becomes beloved precisely for having its own indestructible autonomy and life.

So too, Winnicott notices, a student in the earliest stage of exposure to the field of psychology wants only to know what is expected by the teacher ("Will this be covered on the exam?"). Then, in the second stage, "the student attacks the subject with questions and criticisms, and finds out what's left after the assault; whatever survives this critique—this hatred—is felt to be of real substance (resilient, incorruptible, worth banking on)."[19]

In this way the student is not only transformed by the subject matter but also begins to transform the material and the discipline itself into something uniquely personal and sometimes even unrecognizable to others in the field. Phillips suggests that when we perform this transformation of a subject matter while asleep, we call it a dream; when performed while awake, however, it is "called a misunderstanding, a delusion, or an original contribution to a subject. In other words, in the second stage the student makes the subject fit in with his or her unconscious project," which means, Phillips contends, that "people can learn but they can't be taught, or, at least, they can't be taught anything of real significance. And that is partly because no one can ever know beforehand—neither themselves nor their teachers—exactly what is of personal significance."[20] The student alone—the therapist or preacher alone—must kill the words of the canon to discover what survives.

Phillips concludes from this that the tension inherent in desire and its objects—and possibly reflected in Christian theology's deep ambivalence with curiosity—is that "desire without something that resists it is insufficient, wishy-washy, literally immaterial," but also, "a world that too much resists my desire is uninhabitable, unlivable." The predicament is that "desire is both hope and the impossibility of hope: that the life in us is not always on our side."[21]

A Loss for Words

At the heart of Christian preaching lies a passion story wherein the ultimate Object of human desire—God's very Self humanly embodied—becomes truly real by surviving death itself. Yet this same passion story can become real, therefore healing, for each new generation only by being "killed" again and again by persons or communities seeking to determine what in it survives to become resilient, incorruptible, and worth banking on. This latter killing of the gospel narratives takes place in sermons primarily by means of contemporary passion stories by which to test, critique, or, more powerfully, even hate the biblical text. Although commonly thought to quaintly illustrate the gospel accounts, contemporary stories in sermons serve the far more consequential purpose of embodying or incarnating those gospel accounts by challenging and even "destroying" the biblical claims for God's own passion in Jesus Christ. Without the presence of one or more such stories in every sermon, the central claims of the biblical narratives would remain untested, therefore unreal and unloved for preacher and congregation.

This weightier understanding of their role means that no stories should be included in a sermon merely to amuse, entertain, or fill the dreaded silence, and even less to demonstrate the preacher's own humanness or currency. Rather, the stories are placed there because the preacher has found in them the full intellectual, spiritual, and emotional richness of a partial and particular truth; the preacher, that is, has found them worthy for testing and taking on the gospel truth itself. Like the parables of Jesus or stories revealed by counselees to their therapists, so a sermon's stories from life must not be seen to merely illustrate but to fully embody the honest truth.

Thus, in the privacy of their studies ministers need to be willing to play witness to the mundane squirrel to the place where they find themselves somehow personally overcome by its mysterious judgment, grace, joy, or truth. The preacher needs to pursue an ordinary interest or desire to the point of being threatened by it with sadness, pain, or hope; of questioning prior actions or beliefs; or of finding oneself in tears, or with an irregular heartbeat or sweaty palms, even sexually aroused. Only then might a story win its way into the sermon itself.

The preacher who manages to play witness to everyday life at this rather exacting level of intimacy, however, eventually faces a further complication when, in turn, having to *bear* witness to it in the sermon, for passion by nature resists adequate articulation. Preachers pursue their curious desires not to the point of having a great deal to say about them, but, more poignantly, to the point where words may fail them, to that point of wondering whether they will manage to speak of them at all, of being threatened with a loss for words. Words betray one's passions, so preachers, like counselees, regularly risk humiliation in exposing what matters most to them. Equally troubling, however, is that passions betray one's words, so when speaking their passions, again like counselees, preachers often find themselves bereft of words. Phillips cites John Ashbery: "What moves me is the irregular form—the flawed words and stubborn sounds…that affect us whenever we try [to] say something that is important to us."[22] Like proposing marriage to one's beloved or offering a eulogy for a friend, in the passion stories of a sermon the competent, articulate, adult voice of the preacher sometimes falters and gives way to the preverbal muteness of infancy; in every authentic sermon the preacher may, in this sense, unwittingly and quite literally become like a little child. Language may be the cure for infancy, as Phillips alleges, but attempting to express what most moves a person confounds that very cure. On a regular basis the preacher faces the unenviable task of having to capture in words what at once insists on—yet fiercely resists—eloquent expression.

One practical upshot of this is the advisability of limiting the number of stories from contemporary life included in any particular sermon. One? Maybe two? Rarely more. This economy of stories reflects the limits of the preacher's own capacity for playing witness to life, while also respecting the challenges that confront the preacher when bearing witness to life. Examining fewer stories in their depths rather than more in their shallows enhances the likelihood that each of them will carry its share of the weight of the sermon's truth, healing, power, and grace.

Related to this economizing in terms of the number of stories told is the value of using an economy of words to tell them. When speaking, however discreetly, of one's passions in a sermon (or most anywhere else), saying less is generally preferable to saying more. Even as a marriage proposal or a eulogy should not ramble on, lest the beloved be lost in a thicket of words, so the words of the sermon's exegesis of life should be chosen with precision and care. One indeed witnesses to what one must in the sermon, but to no more. Heeding something of this advice myself, then, I shift now from a discussion of the place of stories in sermons in general to consider more tangibly the function of specific stories in one sermon in particular.

Hearing the Word

The following sermon, like that of the previous chapter, was first preached before a congregation consisting of seminary students, faculty, and staff—this one, however, during a weekday morning chapel service.[23] I based the sermon on a lectionary text for the Sunday immediately following, in what the church calendar traditionally has deemed "ordinary" time. The text tells the dramatic story of Jesus healing a paralyzed young man brought to him by friends undeterred by obstacles. But it spoke to me of certain other kinds of paralysis, as well as of unexpected healing, beyond that of the physical body. The sermon is entitled "The Unreality of God."

■ ■ ■ ■

When Jesus returned to Capernaum after some days, it was reported that he was at home. So many gathered around that there was no longer room for them, not even in front of the door; and he was speaking the word to them. Then some people came, bringing to him a paralyzed man, carried by four of them. And when they could not bring him to Jesus because of the crowd, they removed the roof above him; and after having dug through it, they let down the mat on which the paralytic lay. When Jesus saw their faith, he said to the paralytic, "Son, your sins are forgiven." Now some of the scribes were sitting there, questioning in their hearts, "Why does this fellow speak in this way? It is blasphemy! Who can forgive sins but God alone?" At once Jesus perceived in his spirit that they were discussing these questions among themselves; and he said to them,

*"Why do you raise such questions in your hearts? Which is
easier, to say to the paralytic, 'Your sins are forgiven,' or to
say, 'Stand up and take your mat and walk'? But so that you
may know that the Son of Man has authority on earth to
forgive sins"—he said to the paralytic—"I say to you, stand
up, take your mat and go to your home." And he stood up,
and immediately took the mat and went out before all of
them; so that they were all amazed and glorified God, saying,
"We have never seen anything like this!" (Mk. 2:1–12)*

■ The Unreality of God ■

She was being so unrealistic, and it was beginning to bother
me. The vase sat on the kitchen counter in plain view day after
day, week after week, and she seemed incapable of doing
anything about it. She was paralyzed by love for it, no doubt,
but paralyzed nonetheless, unable to bring herself to do what
we all knew she eventually would have to do.

I was living at the time with this wonderful elderly woman
of considerable means who rented rooms in her spacious home
to impoverished graduate students the likes of me. In her dining
room, standing alone in a reserved space on the buffet under
the gleam of recessed accent lights, stood a vase of Steuben
glass. It was the most beautiful vase I had ever seen. It had a
deep center but then quickly flared out to a wide, flat rim, so
that when she would fill it with fresh tulips they soon would fall
lazily down around the rim, the way of tulips, into a graceful
swirl. I had never thought of lazy tulips as objects of much beauty
before, but in the Steuben they were elegant. She loved the vase
and so did I.

Steuben Glass and I had not been entirely strangers. Even
before I moved into her home I used to take the train from
Princeton to Manhattan every now and again, and I'd walk down
Fifth Avenue with its great stores—Saks, Tiffany's, and the rest,
one marbled exterior after another. Steuben Glass was there
with the rest, and more than once I'd wandered in to gaze in its
darkened rooms, more museum than store. I would gasp at the
price tags: a thousand dollars for this vase, five thousand for
that, ten thousand for the little crystal polar bears. I'd been

exposed to Steuben before, although since we traveled in different social circles this was the first time we were living together up close and personal. You know what I'm going to say next. But it wasn't my fault. There was another graduate student living in that home at the time. One day, when our landlady was out of town for a week and the other student was washing out the remains of some tulips from the Steuben, she knocked it against the sink. A one-inch triangle of glass broke from its rim, and the rest of it cracked from the center of the triangle all the way down to its base. The other student, even more economically destitute than I, could only cry. We left it in all its pathos on the kitchen counter, feeling sick about what had happened.

Our landlady returned, found her beloved vase where we'd left it, and found herself, understandably enough, a little broken as well. She wasn't angry so much as bereaved, and for days that turned to weeks she left it lying there in state on the kitchen counter, unable to bring herself to do the inevitable. "Maybe they can fix it somehow," she would say from time to time, looking for any glimmer of encouragement from me. "You can't repair broken crystal," I'd reply, realistic to the core. And she knew it, too. She was being so unrealistic, and it was beginning to bother me. She was paralyzed by love for it, no doubt, but paralyzed nonetheless, unable to face what we all knew she had to face. Ashes to ashes, dust to dust, sand to Steuben to sand.

■

He wasn't the sole paralyzed one in that room, only the most obvious. His friends, too, were paralyzed in a way, unable to face what everyone knew they had to face. For weeks that turned into months they had refused to face facts, unwilling to hear what everyone kept telling them. The prognosis was worse than grave, the doctors would say; nerve cells simply don't regenerate like other cells. Yet his friends refused to face reality, hauling him from one clinic to the next. "Maybe you can fix him somehow," they'd say, looking for any glimmer of encouragement in the doctors' eyes. "You can't repair broken spinal cords," the doctors would reply, realistic to the core. And the friends knew it, too. They were paralyzed by love for him, no doubt, but paralyzed nonetheless, unable to face what everyone knew they had to face.

You can't help but pity the delusion in their determination to give it yet another try. "He's doing some remarkable things," they'd heard of Jesus. So they loaded up their paralyzed friend and hauled him over to Peter's house, where Jesus was preaching the word that day. If we were talking about people in their right minds they would've given up the ghost as soon as they saw the traffic backed up for blocks. But these were friends paralyzed by love, undaunted by reality, so rather than face facts and turn back they hoofed it instead to the back alley and up the fire escape; and in an inspired act of intercessory vandalism they started digging right through the mud roof of the little house. *They removed the roof above [Jesus]; and after having dug through it, they let down the mat on which the paralytic lay.* You've got to wonder what's going on upstairs with these guys, if you catch my meaning.

For some reason Jesus didn't object to this terrible interruption, perhaps because Jesus himself was never one to be daunted by the facts, never much constrained by reality. Whatever the reason, what happened next was the craziest thing of all. *When Jesus saw their faith, he said to the paralytic, "Son, your sins are forgiven"*—not exactly what the friends were hoping to hear but, on the other hand, not bad, considering what could have been the fallout from their newly engineered skylight.

■

He wasn't the sole paralyzed one in that room, only the most obvious. Early in my ministry I worked for a year as a chaplain in the spinal cord intensive care unit of a hospital in downtown Chicago, where most of the patients were young men my age recently paralyzed by car accidents or athletic injuries or gunshot wounds. It was a frightening place for me to work. It all seemed so senseless, so hopeless, so final. Nerve cells simply don't regenerate like other cells. And in retrospect I think that I, the young chaplain, was likely as paralyzed by it all as the patient who had Frankenstein's bolts screwed into his head.

He was in his twenties, a "complete" injury—medical jargon for a fully severed spinal cord—in the first weeks after his accident. We talked, and he told me about all the things he was going to do to get to walking again, how hard he was going to work at regaining the use of his legs. I knew otherwise, of course, and maybe he himself knew it, too. Since I thought it might be better for him to face the music now and begin to adjust to the reality of his injury, I told him as gently as I could that he wouldn't walk again. Those were the last words he allowed me to say to him.

The young man's father got wind of what I'd told his son and, furious, called up my supervisor demanding that disciplinary action be taken. My supervisor investigated and determined that I had read the chart properly, I knew the facts, I was being realistic with the young man, I was telling the truth; he backed me up and nothing more came of it.

But it's obvious to me now that the young man in this case was right, and that I was wrong. I'm convinced now that my reality was far too small, too arrogant, too petty, too pat. Why is it that we ministers in particular, who collect paychecks by proclaiming the incredible, are of all people so lacking in holy imagination? I'm getting tired of it. I'm sick to death of being paralyzed by reality, and if it came to a choice, I'm beginning to think that I'd much rather be paralyzed by self-delusion. There's something far more attractive to me about my landlady's crazy hopes for her beloved vase, about the determination of the young man's friends to tear out the roof, than all my little certainties put together. If I had been that young man in that hospital, I hope that I'd have thrown me out of that room, too.

■

When Jesus saw their faith, he said to the paralytic, "Son, your sins are forgiven." Jesus' words didn't sit well with some there who could afford courtside seats, some there who kept suffering from a bad bout of realism. *Some of the scribes were sitting there, questioning in their hearts, "Why does this fellow speak in this way? It is blasphemy! Who can forgive sins but God alone?"*

But get this: the scribes were right, realistic to the core—even Jesus must've known that. It's one thing for Jesus to forgive the paralytic if he had committed sins against Jesus himself, but quite another if his sins were committed against someone else. The scribes were right. God alone can forgive those kinds of sins. Yet in an act of intercessory vandalism no less destructive of conventional structures than the inspired mayhem of the paralytic's friends, Jesus razes the roof with his blasphemy, "Your sins are forgiven."

Jesus ripped right through the pastoral professionals' little religious truths, their little social conventions. And when the dust settled and the air cleared he could see furrowed in their faces what was written in their minds. He said to them, *"Why do you raise such questions in your hearts? Which is easier, to say to the paralytic, 'Your sins are forgiven,' or to say, 'Stand up and take your mat and walk'?"* And while we who prefer our little verifiable realities would answer by saying that, well, actually we really would need to see it to believe it, since everyone knows that nerve cells just don't regenerate like other cells, Jesus leaves little doubt that regenerating nerve cells is nothing compared to what he's up against with sin.

The young man on that mat was not the sole person paralyzed in that room, only the most obvious.

■

"I think I'm going to call up Steuben to see if they might not be able to fix it," she said to me one more time. I tried to keep from rolling my eyes. Undaunted by my response, call up Steuben she finally did. She told them that she loved the vase and that though she knew it was crazy, she wondered if they might have some suggestion as to what she might do.

They were so sorry for her loss, they said, but the vase she described was no longer in production. (What had I told her?) But what Steuben said next took our breath away. What they said was this: if she would bring the broken vase up to their store, their artists could fashion a replacement at Steuben's expense. They'd copy and replace it, no charge. Steuben would bear the high cost of what we ourselves had broken.

■

Our realities are so small, yours and mine. Our realities are, "You can't fix broken crystal," or "Nerve cells don't regenerate," or "You'd better turn back since there's such a crowd around Jesus," or "You can't forgive someone's sins unless they've sinned specifically against you." These realities are true, yes. True, but too small.

You see, this was no ordinary vase. This vase was a Steuben. I had failed in my little reality to consider the source, the maker, of this vase. The young man on his mat and the young man in his hospital room were not just paralytics to be dismissed by realistic doctors or chaplains. Each was someone's beloved friend, a father's beloved son, a Steuben, handcrafted from sand by God. So many paralyzed people, paralyzed by realities so deadly because they are partly true. Give me the illusions of my landlady for her beloved vase, give me the delusions of the paralytic's friends, give me the blasphemies of Jesus any day over my pathetic little realities, my pious little orthodoxies. By the time the dust has settled and the air has cleared, you've got to wonder just who the paralyzed in this story really are.

"But so that you may know that the Son of Man has authority on earth to forgive sin"—[Jesus] said to the paralytic—"I say to you, stand up, take your mat and go to your home." And he stood up, and immediately took the mat and went out before all of them; so that they were all amazed and glorified God, saying, "We have never seen anything like this!"

■　■　■　■

Responding to the Word

There are six distinctive sections in this sermon—three of them (the first, third, and fifth) focusing on two different stories from contemporary life (the broken Steuben and the paralyzed young man in the hospital). These alternate with two others (the second and fourth) that exposit the biblical text (the first emphasizes the actions of the paralytic's friends, the second the reactions of the scribes to Jesus). A final section draws a theological conclusion—that Jesus' healing love transcends so-called realities—in reference to the sermon's biblical text and its

two stories from life. These various segments are linked together
by several phrases repeated throughout the sermon, principally,
"paralyzed by love, no doubt, but paralyzed nonetheless," "unable
to face what everyone knew she (or they) had to face," and "He
wasn't the sole paralyzed one in that room, only the most obvious."
This repetition underscores the possibility that paralysis may
be a far more ubiquitous occurrence than those hearing the
sermon may initially be inclined to believe. The sermon depicts
the literal paralysis of the young man in the biblical text and of
the contemporary youth in his hospital room. In addition, it
portrays a kind of paralyzing love or self-delusion evident in my
landlady regarding her vase, in the biblical paralytic's friends,
and in the hospitalized paralytic's father. Finally, it describes a
kind of paralysis stemming from resignation to unhappy
developments perceived as final or absolute, or from unqualified
faith in one's own perception of reality, characterized by the
reactions of the scribes to Jesus and by my actions in response
to my landlady and to the paralyzed young man in the hospital.
Paralysis in these several forms casts a wide and encompassing
net in this sermon.

Beginning in the Middle

In keeping with the specific emphasis of this chapter, the
following analysis focuses less on the sermon's biblical exegesis
than on its "exegesis" of contemporary life. This latter kind of
exegesis begins in this case in the *middle* of a story, in such a
way as to initially disorient ("Who is *she?*" or "*What* vase?") but
in another sense to orient the listener to a theme central to the
rest of the sermon ("She was paralyzed by love"). I typically
begin my sermons with a contemporary story, but it would be
equally acceptable to start instead with an exposition of the
biblical text—though while optimally still somewhere in the
"middle" and quickly establishing even so the sermon's key
theological thrust.

In the sermon's second paragraph, the listener is reoriented
by being brought back to the story's beginning ("I was living at
the time with this wonderful elderly woman"), where both "she"
(my landlady) and "the vase" (a Steuben) are introduced in greater
detail, the vase in particular so as later to heighten the significance

of its loss. I attempt to present my landlady as the sensitive and sympathetic–if here "unrealistic"–person I knew her to be.

The third paragraph ("Steuben Glass and I had not been entirely strangers") serves as a necessary digression to establish for those listeners unfamiliar with Steuben Glass the likely monetary value of my landlady's vase, even as the previous paragraph had established its aesthetic value. This in turn helps to explain in the fourth paragraph the pronounced reactions of the story's players to its having been broken.

The final paragraph in this opening section repeats verbatim the initial theme of the sermon ("She was paralyzed by love for it"), potentially lulling the listener into believing, wrongly, that because the story has come full circle it therefore concludes at this point. Instead, in this sermon and elsewhere, I often present a contemporary story (and also the biblical narrative) not all at once but in parts, beginning at a superficial level of understanding (the amusements and concession stands) but returning later to additional layers of meaning that may offer a surprising twist in plot or allow the story its own timely climax (the mysteries of the sea).

While I do my best to portray my landlady in an agreeable light (e.g., "She wasn't angry so much as bereaved"), the listener is likely to believe that my landlady is the one in need of healing here, an assumption that later developments in the story, of course, will prove unfounded. In the story's initial superficial layer, however, she alone has been the one framed as paralyzed, albeit by love—a theme in turn almost immediately reiterated, again nearly verbatim, in the opening paragraph of the biblical exposition in the subsequent section of the sermon ("They were paralyzed by love for him"). In fact, the opening paragraph of the biblical material in the second section has been anticipated almost word for word in the initial Steuben segment.

The Source of a Passion Story

More important than the foregoing discussion of the mechanics of the Steuben story, however, may be the question of where it came from. How did this story end up in this sermon, linked with this particular biblical text? One obvious answer, of course, would be that it came from my own personal experience, from a memory of an event that had taken place years earlier, long before I began to reflect on it at any length. At the time of the original event, I remember mostly being stunned and a bit chastened by Steuben's decision to replace the vase. It in no way occurred to me at that time to jot down details of the incident to include in my manila file as fodder for some future sermon. In fact, I forgot all about it until the incident suddenly came back to mind, for reasons still mysterious, while I was driving down a highway half a country and five years removed from the original incident.

After I had remembered the circumstances surrounding the Steuben I continued to reflect on them until my next preaching assignment drew near, when I began to consider the lectionary text from Mark's gospel. In only recently having glanced back over the yellow pad with my initial musings on that text, I found reference to the Steuben incident on the very first page. From the outset of my preparation, then, I intuitively sought to factor in the story of the vase and likely read the biblical narrative all along through that particular lens.

It may be tempting to speculate that I had long forgotten the Steuben incident simply because it was insignificant; it was, after all, merely a vase, and one broken not by myself but by someone else. If this had been the case, however, it seems unlikely that I would subsequently remember it at all, and even less likely, when it did finally return to mind, that I would have experienced the accompanying burst of energy that hinted of events insisting on further attention.

A less superficial answer to the question of the source of this story, then, might suggest an original incident experienced less as trivial than, I now believe, as personally shaming. It was unresolved shame, I submit, that was demanding my further attention on the highway that night. At the time of the original events of the story, I certainly felt vicarious shame for the student who actually broke the vase ("It could have been *me!*") and, as I alluded to in the sermon, for my landlady as well ("Why can't she let go of it?"). More disconcerting and therefore recalcitrant, however, was my own mild shame, initially for being glad I was not the one who broke the vase but later for having misread the true reality in this situation. My own expectations had been proven unfounded by this seemingly minor tragedy, surpassed by unexpected grace that undermined my sense of trust in myself. In all likelihood this personal shame was the reason that the circumstances surrounding the Steuben continued to work "underground" within me for so long. Like the vase itself, my own sense of self had been fractured, albeit only slightly, by these events; and, like my landlady, I could no more repair the damage myself than let go of my beloved but compromised self—all of this graphically depicting the insidious nature of shame.

Embracing Shame

In discussing Helen Merrell Lynd's classic work on shame, Donald Capps recounts the usual ways that persons attempt to repair the persistent injury to self caused by shaming incidents—whether by seeking to discount the importance of a shaming event that appears incidental to others but monumental to the shamed person's own sense of self; by attempting to renounce one's shameful self, as in religious conversion; or by seeking to dissociate one's feelings of shame from the original event by intentionally and frequently repeating it, often the case in shame derived from sexual activity. Capps proposes another, more Christian, alternative to these usual strategies, namely, that of embracing and accepting one's shame. "As we cross the boundary from avoiding shame to embracing it, accepting it as the most intimate part of ourselves," he writes, "we create the inner climate in which God becomes revealed to us"[24] —precisely the climate that meaningful pastoral preaching seeks to establish externally as well. Capps refers to the model provided by Augustine's *Confessions* and argues that the most agonizing of the revelations therein expose Augustine's "shameful self and give rise to the pain that accompanies such exposure":

> These experiences were undoubtedly painful when [Augustine] first experienced them. They are more clearly painful to recall to memory now. Thus it often takes him *a long time to begin relating these incidents,* as the details come out in bits and pieces. But he *needs* to recount them, in spite of the pain, because he knows that *as he exposes his shameful self, God is being revealed to him.*[25]

What is the basis for this claim? Capps points to the experience of Jesus' death as that of a common criminal in full public view, a shame

> of the most excruciating kind. Thus to view life from the perspective of the cross, as Christians do, is to embrace our shameful selves, for Jesus' experience on the cross is the paradigmatic shame experience for Christians…To put our shameful selves aside is to dissociate ourselves experientially from the shame of the cross. On the other hand, to embrace our shameful self is to identify with Jesus and thereby experience God as no longer hidden.[26]

Capps quotes Erik Erikson's assessment of Luther, concluding, "Passion is all that man can know of God; his conflicts, duly faced, are all that he can know of himself." Thus, rather than denying or dissociating ourselves from shaming moments where our trust has proven misguided, we need to intensify "our sense of exposure," Capps contends, "for this is the only way we will be able to overcome our sense of isolation."[27]

The self-isolating agony of shame and the urgent desire to expose it is everywhere apparent in Augustine's *Confessions,* but seldom more raw than in his account of the death of an unnamed friend. As a young teacher in his early twenties and living in his hometown of Thagaste, Augustine regularly visited a desperately ill boyhood friend who lay unconscious with fever. When it was determined that he would not recover, the friend was baptized as a Christian. Shortly thereafter, however, he rallied and regained consciousness. At one point in their conversation during this reprieve Augustine made a joke about the baptism with his friend. The friend surprised Augustine by responding to the joke with unmitigated horror, as though, Augustine wrote, "I were an enemy, and in a strange, new-found attitude of self-reliance he warned me that if I wished to be his friend, I must never speak to him like that again. I was astonished and confused, but I did not tell him what I felt, hoping that when he was better and had recovered his strength, he would be in a condition to listen to what I had to say."[28] Before this crucial conversation could take place, however, the friend suddenly relapsed and died. Augustine found himself so disoriented by this series of events that he took flight from the now-strange surroundings of his native town.

That this flight failed to alleviate his shame, however, appears evident in the way Augustine recounts this incident some two decades later. The shame of his youth seems only intensified and compounded in the *Confessions* as the mature bishop struggles there to apologize to God for, of all things, having loved his friend too much: "What madness, to love a man as something more than human!" In seeking, that is, to expose to God the original shame from the events surrounding his friend's death, Augustine unwittingly heaps shame on shame by casting his profound love for his friend as the burning issue. In so doing, he further demonstrates how pathetic and intractable—and how in need of divine intercession—is one's shame.[29]

All of this supports my conviction that it was shame that led the events surrounding the broken Steuben to resonate in my subconscious mind for so long, since those events initially signified for me less God's grace than the limits of my own understanding. It likewise clarifies why, when these events did suddenly resurface, I experienced some urgency to share them publicly— in a sermon, no less—and thus to expose them to the light of God's embrace. The story of the Steuben is one of startling grace, to be sure, but grace distilled from something of my own shame.

A Test of Faith

Shame likewise permeates the sermon's other story from contemporary life, that of my encounter with the paralyzed young man in the hospital. Like the story of the Steuben, my conversation with the paralyzed youth had taken place years earlier, and, like that of the Steuben, I had not previously spoken of it in public. Unlike the story of the Steuben, however, I remembered the paralyzed young man only after I had begun to reflect on the lectionary text, and, unlike the Steuben, the hospital story had no happy ending.

The shame I experienced in that hospital encounter and, to a lesser extent, in recalling it some ten years later was of a more intense variety than that of the Steuben incident, given that the response of the paralyzed young man called into question not only my personal but also my professional identity. That it took twice as many years for me to be able to speak of this event likely reflects both its more threatening assault on my sense of self and its ultimate lack of adequate resolution. The damage to a relationship with a patient whose name I have long since forgotten could not be undone, nor could any damage this encounter inflicted on me. It was, so to speak, a "complete" injury. My effort to be gentle and honest and pastoral with this patient instead exposed me as utterly insensitive and unfaithful; I had been shown to be a fraud in the unmitigated revulsion of shame. Not even eventual absolution from my supervisor, though a welcome relief, could assuage, and may well have exacerbated, my shame in that my need of his rescue further demonstrated my own helplessness and inadequacy.

With its ambiguous ending—the young man remained paralyzed, our relationship never restored and my shame unresolved—this story has a far more acerbic presence in this sermon than does the story of the Steuben. The hospital story more vociferously poses that kind of challenge to the gospel account that Winnicott advocated for students with regard to learning psychology or for adolescents in relation to their parents. The hospital incident begs the question of whether Jesus can redeem its entangled web of paralysis as occurred in the gospel story. The sermon indirectly asks this question by means of this story, but never finally answers it. Instead, those who hear the sermon are left to decide for themselves, and only on faith, whether Jesus can work his "intercessory vandalism" here. The story of the paralyzed youth and paralyzed chaplain, in this sense, kills the gospel account, however stealthily, to determine what in it survives to become resilient, incorruptible, and worth banking on.

Hiding Behind One's Openness

In light of this chapter's plea for pursuing the mundane to its childlike and sometimes shameful depths, preachers need to exercise discretion lest their passion stories in sermons unintentionally increase, not relieve, the burden of shame the listening congregation already carries. There is perhaps no more prevalent theme in my own preaching than that of the transformation of personal shame by God's grace in Jesus Christ. However, I caution against interpreting this to mean that ministers should use the pulpit as a public confessional wherein to seek absolution or acceptance from others for their own shame. It is possible for preachers to hide as much behind their openness as behind their aloofness or guardedness, so that reckless vulnerability in the pulpit may signal the avoidance, not the courageous facing—and owning—of shame. The prominent televangelist or famous actor who begs the forgiveness of a national television audience only days after implication in one or another sexual scandal are only extreme examples of the kind of hiding behind self-exposure that may also occur in sermons.

The lines between honesty and exhibitionism, truth and abuse, and vulnerability and manipulation are dauntingly subtle in vital pastoral proclamation. Preachers might spare themselves and others undue additional embarrassment and shame by pondering in advance whether a particular story elevates their own need for care and healing over that of their congregation. Perhaps another five—even ten—years of subconscious mulling is not too much to ask of them before they enter the pulpit and expose this story's painful truth.

CHAPTER 3

Playing with Strangers

In the previous chapters I have been urging ministers in the early throes of sermon preparation to engage in an introspective process—a kind of uncensored daydreaming—initially centered around a particular biblical text and then around their own pressing (or even seemingly banal) personal preoccupations and desires, a solitary yet intimate practice reminiscent of the method of "free association" in traditional psychoanalysis. In free association, patients are encouraged to lie on a couch and to attempt to verbalize every thought in a stream of consciousness centered around aspects of a recent dream. The analyst, ordinarily seated behind the couch and out of the patient's line of sight, listens intently and with minimal comment throughout the therapeutic hour. Although practiced only infrequently today by dwindling numbers of psychoanalytic purists, free association remains a powerful therapeutic technique for plumbing inner depths and uncovering unconscious desires but also for inviting an experience of unparalleled acceptance or even love.

A historical case can be made for linking free association to creative endeavors such as sermon preparation in that Freud is said to have come upon this method in reading an essay by a German author, Boerne, entitled "The Art of Becoming an

Original Writer in Three Days" (1827). There Boerne advised aspiring writers to "take a sheet of paper and for three days in succession write down, without any falsification or hypocrisy, everything that comes into your head. Write what you think of yourself, of your women, of the Turkish War, of Goethe, of the Funk criminal case, of the Last Judgment, of those senior to you in authority—and when the three days are over, you will be amazed at what novel and startling thoughts have welled up in you. This is the art of becoming a writer in three days."[1]

Anthropologist Tanya Luhrmann, in a recent investigation of the state of contemporary American psychiatry, recognizes something of the emotional intensity unleashed by the process of free association:

> The analytic relationship permits the analysand an extraordinary degree of freedom. Here, for the first time, he is encouraged to say anything—everything—that enters his mind, without worrying whom he might offend or what social mores he might violate. It permits him to say everything and places him in a passive, dependent, exposed position. The asymmetry [of the patient/ therapist relationship] makes the confessor—the patient— feel extremely vulnerable. And the consequence of the vulnerability is a rush of emotion.
>
> The content of those feelings can be wildly varied: hate, love, fear, anger, anything. But the intensity is undeniable and obvious. [T]he analysand tells the secrets of his soul to a person who does not reciprocate, does not respond in kind, and whose face he cannot even see.[2]

While some might critique this approach for its placing the analysand in a one-sided position of vulnerability, Luhrmann was surprised to discover in extensive interviews with psychoanalysts that the emotional intensity of the relationship, in fact, goes both ways. For all of their presumed imperturbability, the psychoanalysts, too, found themselves frequently vulnerable in relation to their patients: "One analyst had a patient so brilliant and so exciting that he had to force himself not to discuss literature; another analyst had a patient who would be one of the greatest writers of her generation; yet another analyst had a patient with such courage that [the analyst] nearly cried explaining it."[3]

In a similar way, ministers who allow themselves unbridled range of expression around a particular biblical text or some other personal interest may come to know something of the rush of emotion or sense of vulnerability of the psychoanalytic patient ("What will God—or the church, or the saints, or my parishioners, or my professors, or my parents, or my fill-in-the-blank—think of me for thinking these things? These thoughts expose me for who I really am!"). The extraordinary freedom to tell the secrets of their souls to a God or faith tradition that does not respond in kind and whose "face" they cannot see places ministers, like analysands, in a passive, dependent, exposed position.

This vulnerability, however, often serves as precursor to a powerful experience of grace. In his book *Pastoral Counseling: The Basics,* James Dittes likens the counselee's freedom of expression in free association to an encounter with God. For brief occasional moments, Dittes argues, the counselee must be able to

> taste the gracious freedom to disregard [her counselor's] reactions and preferences, to jettison all the anxious negotiations with which she has learned to maneuver her way through others' regard, and to bask in the experiment of regarding her own life unfiltered. This can't be unlike the experience of grace that derives from an awareness of a God who is willing to sacrifice self-interest for the sake of an unrelenting benign regard.[4]

Dittes echoes the psychoanalytic conviction that this kind of atmosphere derives chiefly from the counselor's disciplined work of ascetic self-restraint. Only by self-renunciation, Dittes argues, does the counselor invite the counselee into a radically new world where familiar rules of social discourse no longer apply and where a more hopeful construction of self and soul can finally be conceived.[5] By way of contrast, Dittes contends, a counselor's "eagerness to know, to diagnose, to analyze, to prescribe, to manage, to set agendas, to design, to define goals for the counselee and to accomplish them—all this fervor contradicts the affirmation of God's benign sovereignty, is contradicted by that affirmation, and reproduces the conditions that have brought the counselee to feel the need for counseling. These cannot be the components of faithful counseling. They maim and constrict. They harbor idolatry. They offer cheap and unreliable grace."[6]

The opening movements of the process of discovering a sermon thus lead to an emotionally insecure but still enticing inner world where ministers become strangers to themselves. Playing alone with the biblical text and playing witness to life entail, in effect, playing with the stranger within—an often unsettling kind of play where ministers paradoxically come to expect the unexpected about themselves, to know that they do not know themselves. This play necessitates that they allow for boredom—for the desire for a desire—which is to say to allow for their not knowing in advance what unforeseen interest will present itself next and for not preoccupying themselves for the moment with how this strange new concern will ever be incorporated into their more conventional selves. Rather, it becomes enough simply to provide for the dream, to let crystallize their desire.

Against those who might contend that this process would breed narcissistic excess or egoistic sermons, I am arguing that only by encountering the stranger within will a preacher discover a sermon truly hospitable to strangers without. In the words of psychoanalyst Julia Kristeva, "Strangely, the foreigner lives within us: he is the hidden face of our identity, the space that wrecks our abode, the time in which understanding and affinity founder. By recognizing him within ourselves, we are spared detesting him in himself…The foreigner comes in when the consciousness of my difference arises, and he disappears when we all acknowledge ourselves as foreigners, unamenable to bonds and communities."[7] One must wonder whether any outwardly pastoral gesture of welcoming the stranger would not be sabotaged by failing to first face what is strange in oneself.

In his book *God in Creation,* Jürgen Moltmann enlists the
Jewish mystical tradition's doctrine of the self-limitation of God
to underscore the significance of the introspective moment in
creative endeavors:

> In order to create a world "outside" himself, the infinite
> God must have made room beforehand for a finitude in
> himself. It is only a withdrawal by God into himself that
> can free the space into which God can act creatively.
> The *nihil* for his *creatio ex nihilo* only comes into being
> because—and in as far as—the omnipotent and
> omnipresent God withdraws his presence and restricts
> his power. God withdraws into himself in order to go
> out of himself. God does not create merely by calling
> something into existence, or by setting something afoot.
> In a more profound sense he "creates" by letting-be, by
> making room, and by withdrawing himself.[8]

Moltmann likens this withdrawal of God to that of a pregnant
woman who makes space within for the new life she will deliver.
It follows that, far from being selfish or egoistic, the preacher's
attempts to withdraw into self constitute the appropriate and
even necessary early posture for the gestation and eventual
delivery of a sermon.

The two previous chapters may be understood, then, to
provide a framework for playing with text and life such that the
preacher comes also to play with the stranger within. The present
chapter in turn conceives of the third step in discovering a sermon
as one that nudges—or finally permits—the minister to begin to
play with strangers, real and imaginary, without. I initially enlist
as an unlikely ally in this transitional step a reclusive Nobel
laureate with Buddhist leanings—a woman regarded by many of
her peers as the most influential geneticist, some say the most
influential biologist, of the twentieth century and one said to
embody what Winnicott called the capacity to be alone.[9] Later,
I enter again into conversation with disciples of Winnicott, this
time to consider an analogy between sexual or other forms of
perversion and orthodox preaching.

Preparing for the Word

In 1982, Barbara McClintock became the first woman to win an unshared Nobel Prize in Physiology or Medicine. The genetic research, however, for which she received that prize—a discovery called "transposition" in which fragments of genes were found capable of purposeful movement to new positions on chromosomes and thereby of regulating the expression of other genes—had been completed nearly forty years earlier. Beginning in 1951, McClintock had attempted to communicate her findings on transposition to professional colleagues who responded only with uncomprehending silence, baffled by what they considered her mad eccentricity and the unorthodox nature of her claims. Following nearly a decade of unsuccessful additional attempts to communicate her discovery, McClintock simply stopped trying to do so. Instead, she spent her time in almost complete isolation in her laboratory at Cold Spring Harbor on Long Island doing meticulous research—twelve hours a day, six days a week, for fifty years—almost exclusively with corn.

The Single Aberrant Kernel

At the heart of McClintock's genius, her biographer Evelyn Fox Keller concluded, lay a passion for individual difference. McClintock once told Keller, "The important thing is to develop the capacity to see one kernel [of an ear of Indian corn] that is different, and make that understandable. If (something) doesn't fit, there's a reason, and you find out what it is."[10] McClintock believed that the prevailing focus on classification and numbers blinded geneticists of her era to individual difference. "'Right and left,' she says, they miss 'what is going on.'"[11] In their enthusiasm for what McClintock called "counting," her colleagues "too often overlooked the single aberrant kernel."[12]

How did McClintock come to grasp genetic mysteries that eluded others? She did so, she said, by taking time to look, by waiting to hear what the material itself had to say, striving for what she called a "feeling for the organism":

> One must understand how it grows, understand its parts, understand when something is going wrong with it...You need to know those plants well enough so that if anything

changes, you [can] look at the plant and right away you know what this damage you see is from—something that scraped across it or something that bit it or something that the wind did. You need to have a feeling for every individual plant.

No two plants are exactly alike. They're all different, and as a consequence, you have to know that difference. I start with the seedling, and I don't want to leave it. I don't feel I really know the story if I don't watch the plant all the way along. So I know every plant in the field. I know them intimately, and I find it a great pleasure to know them.[13]

McClintock eventually could walk through a cornfield and simply by natural observation of any particular plant determine its precise, peculiar, chromosomal structure; and she never made a mistake.[14]

In 1944, McClintock was invited to Stanford University to assist a friend in his work on *Neurospora,* a red bread mold whose chromosomes were so tiny as to elude all previous attempts to map them. McClintock initially felt paralyzed by this new subject matter and after several days of gazing into the microscope found that she was getting nowhere. She was lost, so she decided to set out for a walk on campus. On a long driveway lined with giant eucalyptus trees she found a bench where she could sit, think, and, she recalled, cry. After half an hour there she suddenly jumped up, eager to get back to the laboratory; "I knew I was going to solve it—everything was going to be all right." Five days later everything was, in fact, resolved.

What had happened? After whatever had transpired under those eucalyptus trees, McClintock said, things began to change under the microscope. Where previously she had seen only chaos, she could now begin to pick out the chromosomes with precision:

I found that the more I worked with them the bigger and bigger they got, and when I was really working with them I wasn't outside, I was down there. I was part of the system. I was right down there with them and everything got big. I even was able to see the internal parts of the chromosomes—actually everything was there.

It surprised me, because I actually felt as if I were right down there and these were my friends.[15]

George Beadle, the Stanford geneticist who had invited her, later remarked, "Barbara, in two months at Stanford, did more to clean up the cytology of *Neurospora* than all other cytological geneticists had done in all previous time on all forms of mold."[16]

When asked how she knew what she knew, McClintock spoke of the limits of rationality: "When you suddenly see the problem, something happens that you have the answer—before you are able to put it into words. It is all done subconsciously. This has happened too many times to me, and I know when to take it seriously. I'm so absolutely sure. I don't talk about it, I don't have to tell anybody about it, I'm just *sure* this is it."[17] She respected complexity and singularity:

Trying to make everything fit into a set dogma won't work. There's no such thing as a central dogma into which everything will fit. So if the material tells you, "It may be this," allow that. Don't turn it aside and call it an exception, an aberration, a contaminant. That's what's happened all the way along the line with so many good clues. If you'd only [put aside your tacit assumptions and] just let the material tell you.[18]

After her death in 1992, James Shapiro of the University of Chicago said of McClintock: "I think the implications of [her] work are just being realized. The idea that…there are systems in the cell that can detect damage and do appropriate things to repair it has tremendous implications for evolution as well as for genetics." In reference to McClintock's reputation for being something of a mystic—a result of her working alone, her emphatic rejection of reductionism, and her clarity of thought— Shapiro suggested that McClintock was more "someone who understands where the mysteries lie than someone who mystifies. She appreciated that the problems we are addressing are enormously deep and complex."[19]

A Provisional Hospitality to Strangers

On about the third day or so of preparing for a sermon, after having already invested several hours alone with the biblical text and in reflection on some current personal interest or desire, I turn from attending more exclusively to the stranger within to listen more intently to strangers without. I begin this process simply by checking the commentaries, typically for me at this juncture a welcome respite from dreamlike introspection. Consulting works of biblical scholars is an essential aspect of the preacher's craft but a task itself not entirely free from perils. Among these perils is the temptation, on the one hand, to capitulate to the perspectives of thoughtful biblical authorities and, on the other, to cling to one's own point of view. Here, Barbara McClintock's grounded wisdom and maverick style provide us both necessary distance and helpful guidance.

In several respects McClintock exemplifies one willing to encounter the stranger within. She herself knew solitude, having been marked as strange and pressed by colleagues into a kind of professional preverbal muteness after many unsuccessful attempts to testify to her childlike intensity of attention and love; her peers believed her to speak gibberish. Despite this rejection, however, McClintock resisted pressures for doctrinaire compliance, unwilling to sacrifice the integrity of her data to the scientific orthodoxy of her day. Averse to knowing in advance what would interest her and pressing her subject matter into preconceived paradigms, McClintock approached her corn playfully, almost sensually—delighting to spend time with it, "befriending" it (down to its genetic constituents), touching it, allowing each plant its own life and history. She attended above all, she said, to the singular and particular in her corn—to the one kernel that was different—rather than pursuing its truth on a grander communal or universal scale ("There's no such thing as a central dogma into which everything will fit"). In each of these regards, McClintock could be said to have modeled the capacity to be alone and confronted the stranger within.

But what of playing with others, with strangers without? Would not McClintock's reclusiveness work against our present effort to move beyond introspection alone in sermon preparation? Did not McClintock essentially ignore others entirely? Certainly ministers who take McClintock's example to heart would trust themselves and their own "take" on text or life over prevailing theological orthodoxies or ecclesial traditions, and when pressed would be apt to privilege the singular, the individual, and the particular over the general, the communal, and the universal. This stance, however, would in no way preclude their collaboration with others in pursuit of creative breakthroughs. The purpose of solitude, I have suggested, is not to promote oneself but, like the self-withdrawal of God or of the pregnant woman, to make space for new relations in community. McClintock's own silence came only after an exhausting decade of being rebuffed in her attempts to converse with colleagues who, to quote Emerson, "declared her ruined"[20] and demanded conformity to prevailing paradigms at the expense of both truth and authentic community. Even then, it seems, McClintock resorted to seclusion less to buttress herself than to protect the integrity of her corn and its revelations; she withdrew herself to make space for an organism unable to defend or speak for itself.

In preparing a sermon, then, I eventually turn to biblical commentaries and other scholarly resources in part to weigh my own pertinent questions and musings to that point against a broader marketplace of ideas. To this end commentators proffer any number of attractive wares: expertise on a text's context or style, perhaps, or on nuances of meaning of key words in their original language, or on one text's relation to others in scripture, or on ways a text has been appropriated throughout church history. I attempt to scan as many different commentaries and other relevant works as possible, jotting down verbatim over the course of an hour or two the most distinctive findings from each—insights that invariably provoke my own imagination and stretch my previous ways of thinking about the text at hand.

Like McClintock's use of a microscope to examine the innermost recesses of her corn, these scholarly resources can serve as penetrating lenses to reveal a text more intricate and complex than that visible to the naked eye. The greater the theological, historical, sexual, racial, or geographical range of these critical lenses—the greater the diversity of their authors' faces—the greater the chances of finding oneself as preacher transfixed by the immense scope of interpretations generated by a single biblical text or particular human circumstance. As Kristeva puts it, "At first, one is struck by [the foreigner's] peculiarity—those eyes, those lips, those cheek bones, that skin unlike others, all that distinguishes him and reminds one that there is *someone* there. The difference in that face reveals in paroxystic fashion what any face should reveal to a careful glance: the nonexistence of banality in human beings."[21] The minister glimpses in others' interpretations of a text a wider world free from monotony.

The peculiarity of the stranger's face elicits not only wonder, however, but also resistance within the observer. On the one hand, its foreign traits illumine one's own face more clearly, perhaps as never before; the stranger, Kristeva suggests, leads the observer to think, *I am at least as remarkable, and therefore I love him.* On the other hand, she argues, the otherness of the stranger leads the observer to conclude, *Now I prefer my own peculiarity, and therefore I kill him.* The foreigner's face, Kristeva writes, "forces us to display the secret manner in which we face the world, stare into all our faces, even in the most familial, the most tightly knit communities."[22]

The "faces" of various scholarly commentators—or conceivably even those faces of familiar colleagues or parishioners with whom a minister might regularly engage in conversation around sermon preparation—evoke a similarly ambivalent thrill and threat. Particularly in perspectives of those from far different stations in life, one comes to see one's own views in startling new light, sometimes for the very first time, while not infrequently also sensing a faint but disconcerting desire to attack the competing points of view (or those who hold them).

The witness of McClintock's professional life underscores this web of ambivalence around exposing one's most personal insights and concerns to others. In embracing what was strange in her corn—the one kernel that was different—McClintock herself came to embody that single aberrant kernel to others; she welcomed the strange while experiencing firsthand the vulnerability of the stranger. By eventually feeling compelled to choose her corn over her colleagues, however, McClintock serves to remind the preacher that earnest consultation on critical matters with diverse others, although essential, remains in itself ultimately insufficient for determining what one must say in the sermon. No outside expert—no commentator, parishioner, colleague, or friend—can finally guide the preacher in this. Genuine hospitality to strangers in sermon preparation does not mean selling them the farm; it does not mean affording them responsibility for what word should be spoken from a particular pulpit to a particular community on a particular day.

In her book *Slouching Towards Bethlehem*, British psychoanalyst Nina Coltart reflects on the conundrums of her line of work, commenting, "It is of the essence of our impossible profession that in a very singular way we do not know what we are doing."[23] Coltart's characterization of psychoanalysis applies as readily to many tasks of ministry, including preaching. Preachers are professionals who get paid for not knowing too much, such that those who do claim to know overmuch (what God would have them say) must be considered suspect. Preachers must, however, know and eventually say *something,* trusting with some trepidation their own sensibilities, informed by playful discourse with diverse and thoughtful others in discovering a sermon within.

Perversion as the Refusal of the Strange

In a memorial tribute to Winnicott's colleague, Masud Khan, Adam Phillips recalls Khan's repeated critiques of the overly interpretive analyst.[24] Such an analyst presumes to know in advance the nature of a patient's difficulties and how best to resolve them. Like the mother who sabotages her child's boredom by suggesting what he should do next, the overly interpretive analyst colonizes and controls, demanding, in Khan's words, "exclusive possession" of the patient and obstructing encounters with anything new or strange. In such a setting the patient continues to remain absent from herself.

For Khan, Phillips argues, the purpose of therapy should instead be to honor patients' silence, to establish a setting where they may become more fully present to themselves. Since Khan believed that persons are always fully present to themselves in their dreams, ideally therapy should take place in a dreamlike atmosphere. He wrote, "Freud intuitively recreated a physical and psychic ambience in the analytic setting which corresponds significantly to that intrapsychic state in the dreamer which is conducive to a 'good dream.'"[25] Just as a mother cannot create a desire in her child but "can only provide the conditions in which it is possible," so the analyst cannot create the dream, cannot bring about the patient's encounter with his unconscious self, but can only set the stage for its emergence.[26]

Having established a suitable context for a good dream, however, the analyst should then remain tentative about the meaning of whatever dream may subsequently emerge; a dream must be only minimally interpreted. Phillips writes: "Freud, as Khan notes, had intimated something of this in a cryptic remark, '[T]hose dreams best fulfil their function about which one knows nothing after waking.'" The analyst's interpretation, like a mother intruding on her child's solitary play, can become a "sophisticated form of interruption, the way the analyst insists on being important" instead of allowing himself or herself to be used by the patient or of becoming "the servant of a process."[27] Psychoanalysis as "an omnivorous interpreting machine," Phillips concludes, becomes just another "colonial adventure" rather than, at its best, "a way of keeping the questions of childhood alive."[28]

Khan believed that excessive intrusion into the dreamlike play of another person actually constitutes or contributes to the development of perversion. Perversion, whether of a sexual or some other nature, is the inverse of a childlike, dreamlike openness to the strange and the stranger within and without. Phillips writes that, for Khan, perversion "is the refusal, the terror, of strangeness—strangeness as signifying difference—in the subtle simulation of intimacy…The pervert, in Khan's version, parodies—or rather, attacks—solitary states of unknowing and imaginative elaboration through compulsive action with an accomplice; and this is done to mask psychic pain."[29] Unlike the "good-enough" mother or therapist, who functions to assist another in sustaining psychic pain, the accomplice in perversion colludes in the denial of such pain, "one collusion being the assumption that it is interpretable, that it can be made into something else…The pervert, however—or rather, someone who uses at any given moment a perverse solution—denies that there is anything new to know."[30]

Perversions, then, are "pre-figurings": "We are being perverse whenever we think we know beforehand exactly what we desire. To know beforehand is to assume that otherness, whether it be a person, a medium, an environment, is redundant; that it has nothing to offer us, that it brings nothing—or just rage and disappointment—to the occasion."[31] Perversions are compulsive, repetitive, collaborative behaviors in service to denying differences between persons or to denying otherness within one's own self.[32] Thus, the pervert becomes "an implicit parody of a certain kind of analyst," one who rather than merely attempting to "witness" what the patient struggles to say instead knows beforehand what it must mean or into which interpretive framework it must be put.

Imagining the Stranger

Khan's understanding of perversion calls into question familiar distinctions between orthodoxy and heresy in sermon preparation and preaching. An orthodox sermon, which I take to include any sermon that expresses what the preacher and listening congregation already know and believe or, worse, what they are supposed to know and believe and that thereby moves toward a predictable conclusion, is by this psychological understanding simply another form of pre-figuring and, therefore, perverse. Orthodoxy betrays perversion, the refusal or terror in its practitioners of strangeness in the subtle simulation of intimacy. The orthodox sermon seduces preacher and congregation alike into colluding in the denial of individual difference and the masking of psychic pain, whereas, ironically, a sermon teetering on the edge of so-called heresy may actually come closer to the mark of an authentic witness to a personal, vital, complex faith and doubt.

I recall hearing a story near the end of what seemed to be a theologically orthodox sermon aired on national television where a distinguished preacher of a mainline denomination told of officiating on the spur of the moment at a ceremony for the renewal of marriage vows of a couple previously unknown to him. The wife later revealed to the minister that the couple had sought to renew their vows as one of a series of dramatic changes they had undertaken in response to the impulsive suicide of their ten-year-old son, "Tom." In the wake of this terrible tragedy the couple had begun to pray and, sensing a growing closeness to God, had become convinced that they needed to do something to symbolize their new life of faith. They decided to completely change their names (including those of their deceased son Tom and his surviving fourteen-year-old brother), sold their farm, and moved to a new region. The woman told the pastor, "I hate to say this, because I know it sounds awful. But there have been times when we've been so happy that we've almost been thankful Tom died in order to bring the rest of us to God." The sermon concluded with the preacher commending the faith of this family that allowed God to make all things new, remarking that he almost cried every time he thought about it.

While I would not wish to dismiss the possibility that God was at work in the aftermath of this family's unspeakable loss, I nevertheless found disturbing the preacher's use of this story in the sermon. Conspicuous in this regard was the preacher's lack of curiosity concerning this unusual series of events. How could he have failed to explore more carefully, initially with the family but subsequently with the congregation (here his television audience), this family's particular response to its multifarious grief? The preacher's negligence had the effect of pressuring the sermon's hearers to collude in what could be viewed as an elaborate refusal of ambiguity on the part of the family and preacher alike. The preacher, in effect, discouraged the possibility of drawing any other conclusions, such as that this couple's actions could be understood as serving to deny their psychic pain rather than as demonstrating exemplary faith.

A subtle subtext of the sermon runs precisely contrary to its more ostensible theme: the way this story was incorporated by the preacher actually constricts the hearers' hopes of God's making all things new, in that they are prevented from entertaining other more complex or ambiguous and, in my view, more likely, possible interpretations of this family's reaction to their grief. The resolutions proposed by the family and endorsed by the preacher come across as potentially simplistic and contrived. The sermon thus risks becoming a calculated refusal of the terror of the strange, a perverse repudiation of the threat inherent in the suicide of a ten-year-old son, rather than a way of keeping the questions of childhood alive or of demonstrating how God makes all things new. Despite its seemingly orthodox conclusion, the sermon has the unintended effect of insinuating that there is finally nothing new to know, that God makes nothing new.

The use of this story in the sermon fails, however, on another less conspicuous but more troublesome front. We have explored earlier how essential is the minister's willingness to confront and embrace the mysterious stranger within and have considered as well how diverse scholarly works provide necessary distance and perspective through contact with various actual strangers without. In addition to these strangers within and without, however, the preacher needs to "confer" with strangers of another kind in the sermon preparation process, namely, those strangers whom the preacher imagines could eventually hear, or overhear, the sermon in its final form. It is this latter type of stranger, I contend, that the preacher in the above case most grievously neglected to consider in choosing to share the story of young Tom's family.

A preacher confronts the intrigue and terror of the strange in part by attempting to imagine how various persons or constituencies within or outside the congregation might interpret and respond to a particular biblical text or contemporary story in ways specific to their own stations in life. The preacher may seek to imagine how a given text would be received by, for example, an eighty-year-old widow, an African American youth, or a divorced father in the congregation. She may ponder what unique questions that she herself may have failed to consider would be raised about a biblical text or story from life by a third-world laborer, an academic feminist or physicist, a Jewish survivor of the Holocaust, a child whose mother has just died, a cancer survivor, or a gay or lesbian person. Anticipating such questions from various possible constituencies lessens the chances that a sermon will enlist collusion in the denial of individual difference or of psychological pain.

In the story of the family whose son took his own life, the preacher neglected and may have even recklessly endangered the lives of one particular group of imaginary strangers who might have heard this sermon, namely, that of ten-year-old boys, and especially of ten-year-old boys from troubled families. How might a young boy from such a family hear a mother's words, "I hate to say this, because I know it sounds awful. But there have been times when we've been so happy that we've almost been thankful Tom died in order to bring the rest of us to God," especially when such words are left dangling, without further elaboration or possibly even condemnation by the preacher? Would it not be reasonable to assume that any spiritually inclined boy with an unsettled home life might pause momentarily on hearing these words to consider whether his own death would have a similarly "redemptive" impact? Would such a boy, I wonder, be more likely to linger on the "almost" or on the "thankful" in the phrase "We've almost been thankful Tom died"? Had the preacher even cursorily taken into account this one obvious community of strangers in this particular case (for what ten-year-old boy would not perk up to attend to this story in a sermon?), it seems inconceivable, absent any deliberately perverse motives, that he would have carried this story into his television pulpit. While it would be impossible in preparing a sermon to anticipate every question, perspective, or objection of every potential listener, the preacher's blatant failure in this instance to consider the needs of children in his congregation could have led to devastating consequences.

The third step in discovering a sermon, then, entails lingering play with strangers—those real and imagined within and those real and imagined without. This step encompasses the thrust of the previous two chapters in encouraging ministers first to look deeply within when considering a biblical text or topic of interest from contemporary life. It presses them further, however, to show hospitality to strangers perhaps far removed from their own personal spheres, to consider what distinctive perspectives others may bring to bear on whatever may be the gospel word struggling to emerge.

Hearing the Word

I offer at this point a third sermon of my own in an effort to explore more concretely the previous discussion on playing with strangers. I delivered the following sermon on the first Sunday in Advent as a visiting preacher to a small, suburban congregation consisting mostly of persons unknown to me. Beyond, in this instance, preaching to bona fide strangers, however, I found myself, in preparing this sermon, encountering strangers of another kind as well—among them my own father and consequently the son I had thought myself to be. The sermon, based on the day's assigned lectionary text of the *Benedictus* of Zechariah in Luke's gospel, was called "A Healing Silence."

In the days of King Herod of Judea, there was a priest named Zechariah, who belonged to the priestly order of Abijah. His wife was a descendant of Aaron, and her name was Elizabeth. Both of them were righteous before God, living blamelessly according to all the commandments and regulations of the Lord. But they had no children, because Elizabeth was barren, and both were getting on in years.

Once when he was serving as priest before God and his section was on duty, [Zechariah] was chosen by lot, according to the custom of the priesthood, to enter the sanctuary of the Lord and offer incense. Now at the time of the incense offering, the whole assembly of the people was praying outside. Then there appeared to him an angel of the Lord, standing at the right side of the altar of incense. When Zechariah saw him, he was terrified; and fear overwhelmed him. But the angel said to him, "Do not be afraid, Zechariah, for your prayer has been heard. Your wife Elizabeth will bear you a son, and you will name him John. You will have joy and gladness, and many will rejoice at his birth, for he will be great in the sight of the Lord. He must never drink wine or strong drink; even before his birth he will be filled with the Holy Spirit. He will turn many of the people of Israel to the Lord their God. With the spirit and power of Elijah he will go before him, to turn the hearts of parents to their children, and the disobedient to the wisdom of the righteous, to make ready a people prepared for the Lord." Zechariah said to the angel, "How will I know that this is so? For I am an old man, and my wife is getting on in years." The angel replied, "I am Gabriel. I stand in the presence of God, and I have been sent to speak to you and to bring you this good news. But now, because you did not believe my words, which will be fulfilled in their time, you will become mute, unable to speak, until the day these things occur."

Meanwhile the people were waiting for Zechariah, and wondered at his delay in the sanctuary. When he did come out, he could not speak to them, and they realized that he had seen a vision in the sanctuary. He kept motioning to them and remained unable to speak. (Luke 1:5–22)

Now the time came for Elizabeth to give birth, and she bore a son. Her neighbors and relatives heard that the Lord had shown his great mercy to her, and they rejoiced with her.

On the eighth day they came to circumcise the child, and they were going to name him Zechariah after his father. But his mother said, "No; he is to be called John." They said to her, "None of your relatives has this name." Then they began motioning to his father to find out what name he wanted to give him. [Zechariah] asked for a writing tablet and wrote, "His name is John." And all of them were amazed. Immediately his mouth was opened and his tongue freed, and he began to speak, praising God. Fear came over all their neighbors, and all these things were talked about throughout the entire hill country of Judea. All who heard them pondered them and said, "What then will this child become?" For, indeed, the hand of the Lord was with him.

Then his father Zechariah was filled with the Holy Spirit and spoke this prophecy: "Blessed be the Lord God of Israel, for he has looked favorably on his people and redeemed them. He has raised up a mighty savior for us in the house of his servant David, as he spoke through the mouth of his holy prophets from of old, that we would be saved from our enemies and from the hand of all who hate us." (Luke 1:57–71)

▣ A Healing Silence ▣

"When I decided to speak I had a lot to say and many ways in which to say what I had to say." These are the words of Maya Angelou, the nationally acclaimed poet, professor, actor, and writer who grew up under the care of her grandmother and her uncle in the forgotten town of Stamps, Arkansas, just down the road from Bill Clinton's boyhood home of Hope. Angelou soared to national attention and acclaim as she read her poem to the nation at Clinton's first inauguration, and her autobiography of her childhood in Stamps, called *I Know Why the Caged Bird Sings,* has remained a bestseller ever since.

I heard her tell part of that same story in a taped interview. Angelou said:

> When I was seven and a half I was raped. The rapist was a person very well known to my family. I was hospitalized. The rapist was let out of jail and was found dead that night, and the police suggested that the rapist had been kicked to death. I was seven and a half. I thought that I had caused the man's death because I had spoken his name. That was my seven-and-a-half-year-old logic. So I stopped talking for five years.
>
> Now to show you how out of evil there can come good, in those five years I read every book in the black school library. I read all the books I could get from the white school library. I memorized James Weldon Johnson and Langston Hughes. I memorized Shakespeare, whole plays, fifty sonnets. I memorized Edgar Allen Poe, all the poetry; never having heard it, I memorized it. I had Longfellow, I had Guy de Maupassant, Balzac, Rudyard Kipling. I mean, it was a catholic kind of reading and catholic kind of storing.
>
> When I decided to speak, I had a lot to say and many ways in which to say what I had to say. I listened to the black minister; I listened to the melody of the preachers, and I could tell when they would start up on that kind of thing when you know they mean to take our souls straight to heaven or whether they meant to dash us straight to hell. I understood it.
>
> So out of this evil—which was a dire kind of evil, because rape on the body of a young person more often than not introduces cynicism, and there's nothing quite so tragic as a young cynic, because it means the person has gone from knowing nothing to believing nothing—in my case I was saved in that muteness, you see, I was saved. And I was able to draw from human thought, human disappointments and triumphs, enough to triumph myself.[33]

"When I decided to speak, I had a lot to say and many ways in which to say what I had to say."

These could have been the words of the old priest Zechariah, for when he finally opened his mouth after his long exile of silence, he, too, had something to say. "Blessed be the Lord God of Israel, for he has looked favorably on his people and redeemed them" is what he finally said, an ejaculation of praise and thanksgiving to the God who had given him both the silence and now the song, given him the terror and now the joy, given him the long life of waiting with his righteous wife, Elizabeth, for a child of their own, and who now in their golden years had given them the son. When Zechariah finally began to speak, he had a lot to say, and what he had to say was *benedictus,* a benediction, a blessing to God on high and to all the people Israel for the great things God had done, the great things God would do through this very child, the one who would baptize the Messiah, who would prepare the hearts of the people for the coming presence of God.

There were too many priests in the neighborhood of Jerusalem, twenty-four divisions of priests named for the ancient priest Aaron's twenty-four sons, some say maybe 18,000 priests in all, so that each division took its turn at serving a week at temple duty just a couple of times each year. There were so many priests that none of them was allowed to offer up the prayers of the people in the temple more than once in his lifetime, and there was no guarantee of getting even one chance at that. But this time the old priest Zechariah had won the lottery of the 800 priests in his division, and his time had come to enter the holy place alone, the one to burn incense on behalf of the many, the culmination of his priestly career. And what an entering, what an offering up it became for the righteous old man!

Once in the holy place, there appeared to him an angel of the Lord, standing at the right side of the altar of incense. When Zechariah saw him, he was terrified, and fear overwhelmed him. But the angel said to him, *"Do not be afraid, Zechariah, for your prayer has been heard. Your wife Elizabeth will bear you a son, and you will name him John. You will have joy and gladness, and many will rejoice at his birth, for he will be great in the sight of the Lord."*

And when Zechariah in his terror—in his realistic awareness of the slim chances of their getting pregnant at their ripe old age—when he questioned this angelic visitor concerning how this could be, Gabriel told Zechariah that he had it on good authority, coming as he had from the outskirts of God's very kingdom. But then Gabriel added that it was too bad Zechariah hadn't believed him right from the start for, because of his disbelief, he would have to be struck mute, unable to speak, until the whole obstetrical miracle was accomplished. So when Zechariah finally emerged from the temple long overdue, the impatient crowd noticed that *"he could not speak to them, and they realized that he had seen a vision in the sanctuary."*

■

A few years ago I was talking with my wife and sister and mother and a few others, and we happened to get on to the subject of my father, who had died several years earlier. It was a good conversation, a lighthearted one, and I remember my sister saying this thing that struck me as accurate, as so much capturing who our father truly was. She said, "Dad never seemed to have to say where he stood, or what he believed, or how we should behave. Without his saying anything and without having to ask you just sort of knew."

I thought as she said it, *Yes, that's just right, that just how he was.* My father was a saintly man, a spiritual man, but he was quiet, so often silent about the big things, the important things. And yet somehow you knew where he stood.

■

Gabriel's penalty for Zechariah seems a little stiff, and you can't help but wonder whether Gabriel went slightly overboard on the discipline out of the angel's own nervousness about this encounter himself, what with the stakes being so high and all— Gabriel's burden of responsibility to set in motion right here and right now the plan on which the whole future of creation was to hang. Nine months of silence for Zechariah seems a rather severe punishment for his having raised a very simple and reasonable question in this traumatic encounter.

Then again, however, maybe the sentence of silence on Zechariah wasn't so much a severe judgment at all. Maybe instead it was something of a severe mercy, a gracious gift for him. Maybe it protected Zechariah from having to say too much too soon, from the ridicule of the community, from others' skeptical disbelief. Maybe it protected the wonder and power of this holy encounter; maybe the silence in some way preserved the mystery of the message. Maybe Zechariah's muteness was the silence of the young Maya Angelou, a solicitous silence, a saving silence, a healing silence, the crucial "white space" on the artist's canvas, the restful Sabbath in the hectic week, that shielded Zechariah as it shielded Maya from their terribly traumatic encounters.

A seminary student whom I did not know came up to me in the cafeteria lunch line the other day and told me about a silent monastic retreat that she'd been on the weekend before. She said she cried for the first two full days of her silence, such was the level of her pain and stress going in.

What if their silence—Zechariah's, Angelou's, this seminary student's—what if their silence was a stillness which would allow them space and time to withdraw from the cynicism of their worlds to emerge at the proper time with wisdom enough to triumph, to emerge with something to say? For when they decided to speak they had a lot to say and many ways in which to say what they had to say.

I, for one, at least, am a little envious of their silence, Maya's five years, Zechariah's nine months, even the student's two days. As one who makes his living speaking words, I often tire of my words; they grow shallow and tepid and worn. I get sick to death sometimes of hearing myself speak—an assessment, I'm sure, with which my students would be delighted to concur—of having to say yet another word about subjects of which I know so little. And I confess there are many occasions when I listen to the words of other priests in their pulpits and utter a little prayer of sorts that God might finally strike them mute, for we preach more often than not from our shallows and not our depths. Would that more preachers could be traumatically silenced for a time so that when they do finally speak they have something to say and many ways in which to say what they have to say.

So maybe Zechariah's silence was not so much an imposition of God's severe judgment but of God's severe mercy, a pregnant pause in the cynicism and tragedy and traumas of this world in which gestates a prayer of wonder and thanksgiving and gratitude in the miracle of new birth, a son named John, a son named Jesus, a redemption and refreshment and restoration of hope and life. A severe mercy, a healing silence.

It took a Steven Spielberg movie for me to get a better handle on my father's silence, to understand it in a new light or, perhaps, in a new darkness. Last year I went to the movie *Saving Private Ryan* in a theater near the town where I had grown up as a boy—a frightening story about the Allied invasion at Normandy on D day and its aftermath in World War II. My wife didn't want to see the film, and I was relieved that she didn't, because even before I saw it I knew somehow that I wanted to see it by myself, all alone.

As a boy of just eighteen or so, my father had fought on the German battlefields of that war, and this was one of those parts of his life he was reluctant to speak about, forever silent about. As a young man myself I remember once screwing up the courage to ask him about his experience in the war, but he mostly dodged the topic, saying that he remembered once getting to ski for a few days during the war in the Swiss Alps and that they were beautiful, that he'd like to return to see them again one day. I asked him if he'd ever killed anyone in battle or seen his friends killed, and he said that he probably had—my father, the quiet Sunday school teacher, the steady Christian.

So I felt drawn to this movie as to few others to help me fill in the blanks of my father's silence, and I was overcome, there alone in the dark theater, by what I saw. After the movie was over, I sat silent by myself for some time in my car in the theater parking lot. And then I drove the few miles to a nearby lake where our family had spent every one of the summers of my boyhood—a lake that had meant so much to my father and me. I sat on a beach close to a cabin that I knew so well. I shed some tears there and prayed to my father in heaven—which of my fathers in heaven at that point I wasn't quite sure. And I began to understand something of my father's lifelong silence, I think, for the first time—as a healing silence, a saving silence, a holy and gracious silence. For what *could* one say in the face of what as a boy he had seen and done?

■

"The greater the crisis the fewer your words" is a morsel of advice I give to my students preparing as pastors to counsel others in trouble. The greater the crisis the fewer the words— the crisis of Maya Angelou, the crisis of Zechariah, the crisis of the seminary student, of my father, of you and me.

But these words I can say with utter confidence: That however noisy and fast-paced, however beautiful the gift wrap and greeting cards, however full of tree lights and glitter we invest this time of year—whatever its glorious and frenetic packaging, the season of Advent is a season of terrible trauma. Whatever our attempts to tame it, we cannot strip from this season its original, overwhelming terror. Zechariah's unbelievably good news was news too terrible to speak; it was somehow in his silence that he was saved, in his silence that he came to have a lot to say and many ways in which to say what he had to say. He was saved in his muteness, you see.

Perhaps we are too eager for God to draw near this Christmas. It has become so simple, so neat, so packaged, so much under our control—God in our box, God on our terms. It's no big deal to welcome a God such as this, just set another place at the table. But where in you and in me is the apprehension, the wonder, the anxiety, the dread and uncertainty, the dumfounded terror and havoc that this coming of God wrought in the lives of the original cast? Where is that in us?

Have we any sense that the good news must be concealed before it is proclaimed, must first be deeply imbibed before it is marketed and broadcast, that the coming of Christ in our midst is no unambiguous event, but a severe mercy, a pregnant pause in the cynicism and tragedy and traumas of this world, in which gestates our prayer for redemption and refreshment and restoration of hope and life? In the silence may be our salvation.

Responding to the Word

This sermon extends to a wider audience a message I have been proposing here especially for ministers: that a living word emerges from a period of childlike muteness, such that the evangelist's task becomes at times as much one of concealing as of revealing its truth. In the following analysis I focus especially on how I sought to take into account both scholarly and imaginary strangers in addition to the stranger within myself in first discovering this sermon.

The Priestly Order of Abijah?

The first text on which this sermon is based contains a number of historical, genealogical, and liturgical details at once integral and yet threatening to obscure the gist of the narrative. It introduces an array of persons and places that include King Herod, Judea, Zechariah, Abijah, Aaron, Elizabeth, and the angel Gabriel and offers as well an involved description of the specific circumstances of Zechariah's family and vocational life. Contemporary persons who read or hear this text for the first time could easily find themselves disoriented or even overwhelmed by its minutiae. What exactly *is* the priestly order of Abijah? How indeed does one *pronounce* "Abijah"? Preachers walk a fine line in needing to offer enough clarifying data to orient the congregation to an intricate text like this without in the process forfeiting the theological and existential impact of what they have found the text to say. The sermon must summarily address and then dispatch any confusion over the text's mundane details in order to provide room for its more compelling concerns.

There are two subsections of the present sermon that focus specifically on the biblical texts. The first of these, coming on the heels of the sermon's opening story of Maya Angelou's childhood silence, bears primary weight for establishing the historical background of the gospel account. Although the opening paragraph of this first expository section sounds the principal existential theme of the sermon ("When I decided to speak, I had a lot to say"), the second and third paragraphs revert to the more workaday task of clarifying the context that listeners will need to more thoroughly embrace the text ("There were too many priests in the neighborhood of Jerusalem"). These latter two paragraphs function to free the subsequent biblical subsection ("Gabriel's penalty for Zechariah seems a little stiff") to focus on what became, for me, the more pastoral heart of the narrative, that of the divine mercy hidden within Zechariah's severe penalty of silence.

Central to our present concerns is the fact that I was almost completely dependent on the works of commentators for understanding the various historical details provided in this biblical account. I could never have imagined my way into the vagaries of the ancient priestly lottery system or the significance for one like Zechariah of offering prayers in the sanctuary of the Lord simply by dreamlike introspection alone. If the two exegetical paragraphs of this particular sermon are, for my own preaching, uncharacteristically detailed, it is because they condense an extended period of study of others' works. My hope, however, is that my own or any commentators' scholarly work will remain relatively transparent in the sermon, never taking center stage or otherwise detracting from the sermon's core trajectory.

Some Other Strangers

Both my own sermon and that of the preacher who told of the family's reaction to their young son's tragic death share a similar theme; both seek to convey that amid traumatic circumstances God works to make all things new. It becomes worth asking, then, whether my sermon falls prey to any of those errors that I critiqued in the other.

Does this sermon provide hearers the freedom to explore, doubt, or question? Does it allow for complexity and ambiguity while still staking a claim for a particular and concrete truth? Does the subtext or structure of the sermon subtly support its message? More pointedly, does a story like that of Angelou's childhood rape and ensuing years of silence manage to circumvent for seven-year-old girls in the congregation the potential trauma for ten-year-old boys of the other sermon's story of Tom?

Those who have heard or read this sermon may be in a better position than I to answer these questions. I can say with some force of conviction, however, that these are the very kinds of questions I hoped to answer in the affirmative in preparing this sermon. I attempted to allow for ambiguity in the sermon, for example, in finding reasonable Zechariah's own doubt concerning the angel Gabriel's revelation. There is ambiguity as well in my repeated use of "maybe" in proposing an unconventional reading of Gabriel's stiff punishment in response to Zechariah's doubt ("But maybe the sentence of silence on Zechariah wasn't so much a severe judgment at all. Maybe instead it was something of a severe mercy"). I provide a glimpse (although one not, I trust, excessively self-revelatory) into my own vulnerability by suggesting that I sometimes tire of having to speak words on behalf of uncertain mysteries or by sharing my reaction to the Spielberg movie and the mystery who was my father.

But what of Angelou and her account of a childhood rape? I have never been a seven-year-old girl, nor an African American living in the old South, nor essentially motherless and fatherless and very poor, nor raped. How can I as preacher imagine my way into the experiences of those strangers in or outside the congregation who may know something of Angelou's world in a way that I do not?

Although Angelou's is not my own story to tell, it is, I finally concluded, hers to tell, and I risked sharing it in this sermon partly because she herself had publicly done so. Angelou does claim that something good has come out this experience in her life while still rightly decrying the rape as a "dire evil." Those who heard this sermon would be unlikely to misconstrue Angelou to be saying that she was in any way grateful for having been raped.

If young girls or others in the congregation had somehow been similarly traumatized themselves, Angelou's self-imposed silence, while certainly not the only or possibly even the optimal response, nevertheless would not likely harm those who attempted to imitate it, and, as Angelou's case shows, could even prove powerfully redemptive. Unlike young Tom's suicide or, in my view, his parents' subsequent attempts to shed their previous identities, Angelou's silent immersion in the words of great literature and preaching could become as salutary for others in the aftermath of trauma as it was for her and as I believe that their silence may have been for Zechariah, the seminary student, and my father. I can say with a certain sense of confidence that times of extended silence, at least for me, have been healing. There is an incalculable difference between a child's hearing in a sermon that a young boy's suicide may have been healing for his family and that same child's hearing that a young girl's silence had been healing for her.

In my own adolescence and early adulthood I found myself wrestling with a phobia of public speaking. Since, in those same years, I had begun to consider entering the ministry and since I knew ministers did a great deal of public speaking, my concerns began to grow exponentially to a point where I became paralyzed not only by the thought of public speaking but also by my anxiety itself. I attempted to face my fears by enrolling in various speech courses and by joining the debate team in school, but in each case I managed to drop the course or quit the team before ever having uttered a single public word. *How,* I wondered, *would I ever be able to preach?*

I am convinced, as it turned out, that I eventually learned to preach less through any speech or preaching courses (which in seminary I was finally required to take) than in large measure by keeping silent. It happened that I attended a college halfway across the country from my home and that, despite the great distance between them, my hometown and college city were connected by a single interstate freeway. I noticed in making that long and monotonous drive by myself many times throughout my college years that I would sometimes remain silent for the entire trip. I could drive for days without ever turning on the radio, but would sometimes listen to tapes of six sermons of a dynamic Scottish minister whose preaching I had once heard and admired. Over the course of those years of driving back and forth across the country, I heard those same six sermons so often that I eventually could preach each of them right along with the tape, word for impassioned word and complete with Scottish accent. I am convinced today that in hearing and memorizing a mere six sermons of a master preacher over extended periods of utter silence, my fears of public speaking were calmed and my present passion for preaching was born. Although I do not share the same traumas of Angelou's childhood past, I suggest by telling this story in conjunction with hers that I respect, with Angelou, the healing power of words carefully crafted and reverently absorbed in periods of long and measured silence. In this way, perhaps, she and I may not be strangers at all.

CHAPTER 4

Playing with Fire

In her study of cultural collisions between Hmong immigrants to the United States and Western medicine, journalist Anne Fadiman captures something of the drama and tension of life at the boundaries. She writes: "I have always felt that the action most worth watching is not at the center of things but where the edges meet. I like shorelines, weather fronts, international borders. There are interesting frictions and incongruities in these places, and often, if you stand at the point of tangency, you can see both sides better than if you were in the middle of either one."[1] It is primarily at such boundaries, Fadiman contends, that one experiences the simultaneous threat and promise of finding something new.

The present chapter brings the preacher to another such pivotal place, where the often incongruous individual pieces of the process of discovering a sermon inevitably meet, collide, and come together as one. The preacher here begins to tinker with odd and sometimes volatile combinations at the edges of the mundane and the sacred in formulating contemporary parables that fuel a sermon. At their most electric, such parables, like the clashing of atmospheric fronts (and not unlike Jesus' own parables), generate a torrent of heat and light. Having played already with text, with life, and with strangers, the preacher comes finally to play precariously with fire.

Preparing for the Word

How are adolescents floating naked in a pool like the ascension of Jesus into heaven? How are these, in turn, like an anxious young man on his first day at seminary or overcome by the wealth of Brazilian poverty, or like a puppet frog singing of rainbows? What have Jesus' confrontations and healings to do with the breaking of a costly crystal vase or with a hospital chaplain's costly missteps with a patient? How is the infant Jesus' coming into the world or the silencing of an impotent priest like the aftermath of a young girl's rape or like a son encountering his father's wartime past?

One senses a tangible threat inherent in thinking, but especially in voicing, such questions as these—the threat of trivializing the holy, of glorifying the commonplace, or of being held responsible for unleashing on the world some freakish distortion of what is truly human or divine. Despite the consternation they often provoke, however, such questions constitute the raw material for parables, poetry, even political cartoons, as well as for significant breakthroughs in most every field of creative inquiry. They prove themselves no less essential to the preacher's own craft: "The kingdom of heaven is like…; the kingdom of God is like…"

Preachers, of course, have long made use of contemporary parables in their sermons. What may be unconventional in what I am proposing, however, is the sense that these parables can, even must, be created from individual components that on the surface seem to be in no way obviously related, which may be another way of saying that parables are fashioned not at the center of things but where the edges meet. The most personally powerful (and in my view, homiletically effective) breakthroughs of all in discovering a sermon emerge from placing on a collision course whatever may be the preacher's current preoccupation or desire with whatever may be the assigned or selected biblical text of the day: *any* interest or desire—black squirrel or skinny-dipping youth or Steuben vase—commingling with *any* biblical text, rather than some supposedly viable illustration derived from a preacher's preconceived notion of what a text or tradition is believed to say. In terms of the power or truth of a particular sermon, it would make no difference whatsoever whether the story of, for example, the Steuben vase, initially paired with the narrative of Jesus' healing of the paralytic, were instead to be linked with Zechariah's revelation in the temple or with Jesus' ascension into heaven. Similarly, the story of the aftermath of Angelou's rape or of my journey through the Brazilian shantytown might be as fruitfully joined to any one of these same biblical texts. Any of these combinations would make for stimulating, though in each case very different, insights into the texts at hand and for equally revealing, though again quite dissimilar, sermons.

It is of lesser concern what story is wed to what text than that both story and text are found to be interesting and meaningful and are subsequently engaged at a level of sufficient depth that the preacher himself becomes affected—challenged, delighted, inspired, convicted, aroused, transformed—by them. Radically, the edges of *any* story of interest to the preacher can be productively engaged at the edges of *any* biblical text. Thus, the preacher never again needs to go hunting for an illustration appropriate to a given passage of scripture. Instead, any and every story truly of interest to the preacher is one fitting for the day's assigned or chosen text, assuming again that each is engaged at a level of existential depth where lie submerged the mysteries of the sea, rather than at that of the boardwalk with its amusements and concession stands that everyone already sees.

Creativity or Abomination?

In an article entitled "Abomination and Creativity: Shaking the Order of the Cosmos," Carol Lakey Hess, like Fadiman, underscores that the act of bringing together two previously disparate elements, a process Arthur Koestler once called "bisociation," can lead to an explosive flash of creative insight, but as likely to an explosive threat of moral abomination.[2] Both creativity and abomination, Hess contends, are rooted in a similar metaphoric process: Both bring together two images or ideas that previously seemed incompatible; both disrupt familiar ways of seeing, thinking, or acting; both threaten the established social order.

Robert Oppenheimer, the American physicist who oversaw production of the first atomic bomb, proposed that the code name "Trinity" be used for its initial test detonation. "Alluding to the fourteenth of John Donne's Holy Sonnets, where the 'three person'd God' is said to 'breake, blowe, burn and make me new,'" Hess writes, "the scientist associated the theme of redemption through destruction with the intended work of the bomb." Here, Oppenheimer's bisociation attempted to transform death into something divine. But can his imaginative act, Hess wonders, truly be considered "inspired"? Is it not instead an abomination?[3] Much is at stake and much pain is often involved in distinguishing creative new insights from mutant moral abominations. She writes:

> As an imaginative exercise, comparing a church to a tavern may seem rather harmless. However, if this question ["How is a church like a tavern?"] were posed in the context of moral deliberation, the situation would become more volatile. What if the responses to this question were to influence church confession and practice—such as serving the sacraments, church discipline, or the ordination of clergy? Then [the bisociation of church and tavern] could lead to profound communal conflict.[4]

The church continually finds itself embroiled in just such a crucible of moral deliberation, and sermons are prepared and delivered in this very context for this particular purpose. While the truth in such deliberations is seldom obvious and the outcomes of these struggles seldom definitive, the church is nonetheless called to straddle the discomfiting border between creativity and abomination. Indeed, Hess argues, God's own activity in the world is precisely that of creative abomination, of shaking the order of the cosmos:

> To Hellenistic thinking, the conjoining of an infinite, immutable God with an imperfect, corruptible, and finite flesh was an abominable notion. To go further and claim

that this incarnate God became tainted with and perished under the disgrace of criminality was a "scandal," an abomination, "a stumbling block" to some and "foolishness" to others (1 Cor. 1:23). To religious thinking, the unimpressive prophet who overturned distorted tradition and associated with unclean persons was a blasphemer. And yet, to those who had "eyes to see and ears to hear," the advent of God in human flesh was a miraculous source of new life and a new order of being. The Gospels reveal that prostitutes understood Jesus more clearly than his disciples; a disciple sold himself more deeply than a prostitute. The biblical understanding of grace often threatens our understanding of the order of things.[5]

While there is a place in our lives for moral outrage, Hess concludes that there must remain room as well for testing our revulsions, since what may seem to us initially abominable and fill us with disgust not infrequently signals the creative activity of God's grace in our midst. "This side of the eschaton," Hess writes, "we will not escape the need continually to open our judgments *and* judge our openness" in attempting to live amid the "scandalous order of God."[6]

The Old Story and the New Song

Every preacher in every pulpit stands astride this unstable fault line at the incendiary point of tangency between creativity and abomination, between comfort and affliction, between, as the familiar hymn puts it, the old, old story and the new, new song. By the time a minister actually begins to write a sermon, the number of voices vying for attention is formidable. It includes a carefully considered scripture text or two, the preacher's own examined interests or desires, commentators and other strangers, as well as the press of liturgical seasons or other pastoral occasions that often need factoring in (Is this sermon for a wedding or funeral? in the season of Advent or Pentecost? attendant to a baptism or the Lord's supper, or to receiving new members or ordaining new officers?). How can one as preacher bring coherence to this cacophony of concerns?

The answer, perhaps frustrating, is by the preacher's getting out of the way, allowing those several dissonant voices to negotiate their own unpredictable accord. The preacher seldom knows in advance what kinds of turns a sermon will take or what conclusions will be drawn, apart from the often painful process of actually writing it. A sermon's coherence seems to emerge quite removed from, and not infrequently contrary to, the preacher's own intentions, as words, sentences, and paragraphs slowly find their proper place on the page or screen. The preacher's own role in this puzzling exercise primarily entails sitting for long hours and picking up a pen or pecking at a keyboard until the various voices finally rejoin to say what they will say. As Gardner Taylor, quoting Paul Scherer, put it in his 1976 Beecher Lectures, "Inspiration is 10 percent genius and 90 percent firm application of the seat of the pants to a chair."[7]

The practice of getting out of the way of one's material, an intuitive art more than an exact science, probably needs to be "caught" more than taught. Although I cannot fully explain it and though it remains for me almost always disconcerting, so frequently have I experienced what may best be described as being written *by* a sermon even while I am writing it that I now simply attempt to respect the sermon's own insistent claims on me. I try to maintain a playful trust and childlike openness not only at the earliest stage of the preparation process but also as I begin to write. I resonate in this with Michel Foucault, who in an interview not long before his death noted, "The main interest in life and work is to become someone else that you were not in the beginning. If you knew when you began a book what you would say at the end, do you think that you would have the courage to write it?"[8]

So, too, William Stafford, a prolific American poet, observed about the process of writing that we can all

> learn technique and then improvise pieces of writing again and again, but without a certain security of character we cannot sustain the vision, the trajectory of significant creation: we can learn and know and still not understand. Perceiving the need for that security of character is not enough—you have to possess it, and it is

a gift, or something like a gift. You can't earn it, or calculate how to get it. But it may come, when you enter the life of writing with patience and trust. Dawn comes, and it comes for all, but not on demand.[9]

What Stafford claimed for the life of the writer in general seems especially applicable to one who writes of sacred things in particular: that a "writer is not so much someone who has something to say as he is someone who has found a process that will bring about new things he would not have thought of if he had not started to say them."[10]

"For me," Stafford affirmed, "an artist is someone who lets the material talk back."[11] Resisting those who think of writing— and especially, we might assume, of sermon-writing—"as if it's penmanship," as if it were the practice of taking "dictation from your psyche that has already done something," Stafford instead focused on "the psyche that hasn't done something and then does something." He wondered, "What does [the psyche] do in between?" He therefore always tried, he said, to get prospective writers "to relax enough to pay attention to the things that actually occur to them during the process of writing" itself,[12] advice that may also encourage preachers, still uncertain of precisely where their sermons will head, to sit down to write.

Encircling the Cross

To help me envision just how the edges of multiple and often complex narratives might begin to come together in a single sermon, I sometimes draw on my yellow pad a large circle or pie chart usually divided into four or more sections. One section represents the biblical text, another a contemporary narrative or personal interest, a third the liturgical season in which the sermon will be preached, and the last section or sections any special pastoral occasion (a funeral, baptism, or catastrophic political event, for example) or peculiar local concern that must also be taken into account. I then, in turn, draw a smaller circle at the center of the larger one, this one representing a space where these many pieces of the pie meet as one.

I have frequently found that the place in my own life where the edges of the sacred and profane most fluidly merge is in the image of the cross of Jesus of Nazareth. I often attempt to imagine at this point how that cross would aid in uniting the disparate factions composing the various sections of the circle. To reinforce this point graphically, I sometimes draw the symbol of a cross there within the small inner circle on the page.

At one time in my preaching I took as prescriptive the apostle Paul's declaration that he preached only "Jesus Christ, and him crucified" (1 Cor. 2:2), making sure to somehow include explicit reference to the cross in every sermon. Paul's counsel regarding cruciform sermons remains persuasive for me today, and the events surrounding the passion of Jesus continue to ground my own experience of faith. If anything distinguishes Christian preaching in speaking to the pain and shame of each new generation, it is the embarrassing particularity of Jesus naked and ashamed on his cross. Despite ardently clinging to this precept, however, and for reasons I do not fully understand—whether because at times even Jesus' cross can become numbingly familiar or a sermon's trajectory too clichéd—I now find myself increasingly willing to allow other, still christocentric, stories and symbols to share with the cross their own moments in the sun.

On Not Mixing Metaphors

One additional word of practical guidance: a parabolic approach to discovering a sermon requires that preachers clarify in their own minds how each specific component or player in one complex narrative correlates to each specific component or player in the other. At some early point in writing the sermon on Jesus' healing of the paralytic, for example, I had to determine who in the biblical narrative—whether the paralyzed youth, the friends who carried him, Jesus, the scribes, or the observing crowd—would best be identified with the broken Steuben vase, and who in turn with the Steuben Glass company, with my landlady, and with my own role in the story. So too, in the Advent sermon on the silence and song of Zechariah, I had to ask myself who among the players in the biblical narrative would best be paired with what specific persons in Angelou's account of her childhood rape and with what figures in the account of my own father's silence as well. The preacher, in essence, becomes here a casting director assigning actors to their various roles in the play. Who will play what part? The preacher personally unable to clarify these metaphorical links after long hours of grappling with competing narratives in private cannot expect members of a worshiping congregation to be able to do so in their mere few moments of hearing a sermon in public.

Returning then to the earlier example, I as preacher, at some point, had to decide that for one particular sermon the Steuben vase would be aligned with the paralyzed youth on his mat, even though it would be possible to conceive of other sermons in which the broken Steuben could as effectively represent, for example, the friends who delivered him or even Jesus himself broken on the cross. So too, in the other previous example, I at some point determined that for this particular sermon Angelou in her childhood trauma would always characterize Zechariah in his encounter in the temple, and so on down the line as I meted out assignments for every other major player in each of the sermon's chosen narratives. In any given sermon, then, the preacher must take care to assure that these metaphorical connections, the players' assigned roles, though usually transparent in the sermon itself, nevertheless remain seamless and consistent.

Hearing the Word

We turn at this point to another sermon, this one preached at a daily morning chapel service before a seminary community in the rural Midwest. I based this sermon, like the previous ones, on an assigned lectionary passage that, in this case, included Jesus' teaching on divorce. Knowing that I would be preaching to many who had been divorced, as well as to many children of divorce, and also to others who would be on guard for whether I would equivocate on Jesus' hard words, I sensed in preparing this sermon something of what preachers may experience as playing with fire. That the lectionary text also included Jesus' blessing the little children and that this worship service was to include the sacrament of the Lord's supper further compounded the complexities. I drew the sermon's title, "Gift of Finest Wheat," from the refrain of a contemporary hymn that begins, "You satisfy the hungry heart with gift of finest wheat,"[13] which came to mind while I was contemplating the sermon's primary contemporary narrative and which, I decided, the congregation would sing during the communion service that followed.

Jesus left [Capernaum] and went to the region of Judea and beyond the Jordan. And crowds again gathered around him; and, as was his custom, he again taught them.

Some Pharisees came, and to test him they asked, "Is it lawful for a man to divorce his wife?" He answered them, "What did Moses command you?" They said, "Moses allowed a man to write a certificate of dismissal and to divorce her." But Jesus said to them, "Because of your hardness of heart he wrote this commandment for you. But from the beginning of creation, 'God made them male and female.' 'For this reason a man shall leave his father and mother and be joined to his wife, and the two shall become one flesh.' So they are no longer two, but one flesh. Therefore what God has joined together, let no one separate."

Then in the house the disciples asked him again about this matter. He said to them, "Whoever divorces his wife and marries another commits adultery against her; and if she divorces her husband and marries another, she commits adultery."

People were bringing little children to him in order that he might touch them; and the disciples spoke sternly to them. But when Jesus saw this, he was indignant and said to them, "Let the little children come to me; do not stop them; for it is to such as these that the kingdom of God belongs. Truly I tell you, whoever does not receive the kingdom of God as a little child will never enter it." And he took them up in his arms, laid his hands on them, and blessed them. (Mk. 10:1–16)

■ Gift of Finest Wheat ■

It was a bitter harvest indeed. On most of the farms in the Ukraine region of the former Soviet Union where the American seed corn was planted, no corn grew at all, although twenty tons per acre had been promised. Unlike Hallmark greeting cards that we're told to send when we "care enough to send the very best," in the case of the American agricultural products corporation Zeneca, which in 1993 agreed to sell surplus American corn seed to the Ukraine, we cared so little as to send our very worst.

The Zeneca corporation sold 200,000 bags of corn to the Ukraine, an area with the world's richest soil but a shortage of seeds due to the collapse of communism. Zeneca officials argued that they had given "the best we had," but American farmers assisting the Ukrainian government begged to differ. For one thing, much of the Zeneca seed was of a kind to be planted where the growing season exceeded 100 days, but the growing season in the Ukraine is shorter than that. "Not only were the seeds inappropriate, but many were also bad," according to the American farmers there. "Some were so moldy that it appeared they had been rotting in a warehouse for some time."

"It's a very [bleak] page," said David Sweere, a Minnesota farmer serving as chairman of the agriculture committee of the American Chamber of Commerce in the Ukraine. "There was a time when the Ukrainian farmer held the American farmer in very high regard. Now, they have lost respect for us, because of deals like this. Yes, we in the West believe in commercial gain. But if that is your only goal, then this is what happens."[14]

■

The funny thing is, what we can get away with is so much *less* than what we could actually have. Zeneca got away with its sale of rotten seeds, its $70 million in the bank. But what it got away with was so much less than what it actually could have had in its relationship with the Ukraine.

■

Jesus must have known that no answer he could give would satisfy his questioners. Any answer at all on the Pharisees' own terms would lead only to an endless series of additional clarifications on this or that fine point of the law, until the victim—Jesus in this case—must finally collapse in exhaustion or lose control in frustration, either reaction one in which the Pharisees, to be sure, would have taken enormous delight.

So when the Pharisees came to Jesus to inquire of his position on the current theological debates concerning divorce, Jesus refused to engage the question on their terms. Instead of wandering into their jungle of jurisprudence or into libations of legalese, Jesus answered their question in terms of grace, of gospel, in terms of what God hopes for us to have. The question for Jesus was not so much one of what legally we can get away with, how far we can push the envelope, the limits of the letter of the law. No, for Jesus the question was one of what good things God desires for God's children, what gracious aspirations God has for God's people.

The Pharisees, trying to test Jesus, remind him that *"Moses allowed a man to write a certificate of dismissal and to divorce [his wife]."* Moses says that we can get away with it. But Jesus refuses to enter this quagmire of defining down to the minutiae what is legally permissible and instead talks about what God desires. He responds, *"From the beginning of creation, 'God made them male and female.' 'For this reason a man shall leave his father and mother and be joined to his wife, and the two shall become one flesh.' So they are no longer two, but one flesh. Therefore what God has joined together, let no one separate."*

Do you hear the difference, the distinction between what the Pharisees ask and the way Jesus responds? The Pharisees ask for what is allowed concerning *divorce,* but Jesus speaks of what God desires for *marriage.* It's the difference between divorce proceedings and wedding ceremonies, a difference of night and day. Divorce is grounded in law, marriage in gospel. Yes, you can get away with divorce, but what you can get away with is often so much less than what you could actually have, than what God intends for God's beloved.

The Pharisees try to trap Jesus by quoting scripture to him, by making him disagree with Moses' teaching on divorce in Deuteronomy 24: *Moses allowed a man to divorce his wife.* But Jesus trumps their trap by quoting scripture himself, a practice we may want to keep in mind when some in our midst use scripture to isolate and condemn those who stand apart from the crowd today. There is a word in scripture even more precious than the law of Moses, Jesus is telling them, and that word is the gospel of God, a word of God's good creation, whereby *God made them male and female,* intending for them and for us life and freedom and intimacy, not death and brokenness and despair.

Jesus is no fool. He knows that marriages end, that promises get broken, that love sometimes sours and dies, that abuse and violence and poverty and even wealth all take their toll. He knows that divorce happens and probably always will. And he knows that we can get away with divorce, if we have to, if it has to be. What, is God going to stop loving the divorced or something? But Jesus' focus is elsewhere. He knows there's a big difference between what we can get away with and what we could actually have, and when pushed into a corner, he comes out fighting for life, for grace, for creation, showering us with friendship and romance and goodness and love.

■

You're beginning to sense by now that I'm talking here about something other than divorce alone. It would be easy for those of us who are not divorced to stand smugly in our pulpits or sit securely in our pews thanking God that we are not like those around us who have failed so miserably in marriage. Rather, I think we should be grateful for divorced persons in our midst, for they know far better than most what it is to live not by works, by what they can get away with, but by the grace of God, who rescued them in the painful separations and losses of love and life. It is the divorced who know better than most that Jesus is right, who know in their own flesh and blood that divorce is the last thing God intends for human beings to suffer, the last thing God desires for human relationships. It is the divorced among us who know in their souls that the sound of a judge's gavel did not end the relationship with their marriage partner, but that a marriage of sorts continues ever afterward and that indeed what God has joined together no one, neither judge nor attorney nor extraneous lover, can ever render asunder.

And it is the divorced who know more than most that divorce can be a sign of repentance by which two people finally face up to their failure, that it can be a confession that they have not succeeded in living according to God's will, that divorce can be what finally sets them free to experience anew the extravagant mercy of God. It is the divorced who know only too well that the preservation of outward appearances of marriage when the inner marriage is dead can be hypocritical and self-deceiving, that there is something more righteous even about divorce than living one's life as a lie. Divorced persons know these things deeply within and could likely teach the rest of us a thing or two about what it means to live by grace alone.

But I think this passage is teaching us, finally, about something more than divorce. Rather, I think its message goes something like this: that while you and I so often settle for measuring our lives by what we can get away with, comparing ourselves to the shabby piety of our neighbors and feeling quite self-secure, Jesus instead wants to show that there is so much more God has in mind. Not more rules and regulations, not more guilt and shame, but more wonder and beauty and desire and love. Jesus is trying to tell us over and over again that while we seek to survive on our meager gruel of morality and propriety, God instead has prepared a celebratory banquet of acceptance and freedom to delight and satisfy our famished souls. While we go on debating the finer points of spiritual rectitude and church order, whether God will get us for divorce or for this or that or the other thing— while we go grubbing for our little scraps, God is arranging the flowers and polishing the silver, patiently setting the table for a feast the likes of which we have never seen or dared even to imagine. What we can get away with is so much less than what we could actually have.

I traveled with a group a few years back to what was then the Soviet Union, and we were told to bring for our Russian hosts little gifts of toiletries or cosmetics or other items difficult to come by over there. One of the suggested items was disposable razors, which I happened to mention shortly before the trip to the woman who was cutting my hair. She replied, "Oh, I have hundreds of BIC razors in the back room that I can't get rid of. None of my customers like them. You're welcome to take those." I told her that I'd never liked BICs either—they make the head too big or something, and I always cut myself with them—so I turned down her offer and decided to buy some packages of the kind of razors I used, Gillettes, I think, instead.

Once in the Soviet Union, I asked one of our Soviet guides whether he needed any razors. You won't believe his reply. "Are they BICs?" he asked. "I don't want them if they're BICs, because they cut my face." I couldn't believe it! He knew about BIC razors. And I was happy to be able to tell him, "No, I don't like BICs either, so I brought these Gillettes, the kind I use."

■

The Zeneca corporation got away with sending gifts of rotten seeds. I probably could have unloaded hundreds of countenance-scarring BICs. And yes, we probably can get away with divorce, if it comes right down to it. But the point of our existence is not merely to skate by, not simply to get away with something, the least we can share, the most we can scavenge and still sneak into God's favor.

God's economy is not based on getting by. It has never been based on laws of scarcity, of supply and demand, of survival of the fittest, of "There's a sucker born every minute." No, God's economy is based on overflowing abundance for you and me, for every one of God's little children. "[Jesus] took [the little children] up in his arms, laid his hands on them, and blessed them." There was enough of him even for them, room at the table even for them.

If anyone could get by with sending less than the best, God could get by. If anyone has reason to say, "Send them the rotten seeds, give them the BICs"—if anyone could talk like that, God could. But friends, God's economy is based not on skimping by, not on keeping the best for God's own self, not on doling out divine scraps and leftovers, whatever it is that won't cost God very much. God's economy is based not on law but on love, not on balanced ledgers but on extravagant excess, not on meager portions of gruel but on the gift of finest wheat, not on judges' gavels but on rose petals strewn before a beautiful bride's feet, not on keeping us away but on taking us up into arms that bless and keep us, you and me and all the little children of God.

How can I know? How can we be certain?

I can only be sure, I think, because of Jesus Christ, the very best God cared to send. When I look at Jesus, outwitting Pharisees or scooping up children, when I look at Jesus, his body broken, his blood outpoured, I think I can believe, at my better moments anyway, that I will be OK with God, that God's righteousness is exceeded only by God's mercy and love, that my inadequacies and failures, my living lie of a life, my striving and foraging to satisfy my hungry heart, my fears of doing right and my fears of doing wrong—only when I look at Jesus do I find a little hope that I will be OK, that everything will be all right, the one whom God cared to send when God cared to send the very best. No rotten seeds, no unsold BICs, no table scraps, but an only Son, the bread of life, the cup of salvation, the gift of finest wheat.

■ ■ ■ ■

Responding to the Word

This sermon strikes me as somewhat different in tone from the previous ones, perhaps more in keeping with topical sermons often considered a mainstay of pastoral preaching. It focuses at length, to be sure, on the topic of divorce, a matter of considerable significance and frequent emphasis in traditional pastoral preaching and one of understandable concern to many pastors and parishioners alike.

Despite this semblance, however, I would argue that this sermon distinguishes itself in some important respects from the more familiar and, in my view, less vital topical approach. Unlike the usual starting point in topical preaching, for example, I did not first decide that my congregation or I would benefit from a sermon on divorce and then go hunting the scriptures for a suitable text. Instead, I chose to use the lectionary gospel for this sermon just as in most others. Insofar as this sermon focused, even at some length, on the topic of divorce, it did so because a respectful consideration of this difficult passage insisted on it.

In preparing this sermon I recall thinking that only persons who were married or divorced, or whose parents were divorcing or had divorced, would likely be interested in a sermon that focused almost exclusively on divorce. While this umbrella would cover a sizeable portion of most contemporary congregations, I hoped to discover how the text could speak to an even broader audience, one that would include persons who, like myself, might have had little firsthand experience of divorce but who nevertheless might have good reason to consider their own lives in light of Jesus' teaching on the subject. To have concluded that this text is only about divorce or to have preached from it an essentially topical sermon on divorce not only would have led a significant minority of the congregation to tune itself out, but also would have been reductive of more complex dynamics in the narrative.

The sermon further differentiates itself from a topical one in that its central theme, that "what we can get away with is so much *less* than what we could actually have," would not have emerged, I submit, apart from my attempt to discover how Jesus' hard teaching on divorce might converge with what for me at the time was a disheartening newspaper account of the failed corn harvest in the Ukraine. At the outset it was not at all obvious to me what connections, if any, might surface in juxtaposing Jesus' teaching on divorce with the narrative of a grain sale gone sour. The result, for ill or gain, was a sermon that veered off the beaten path of the topic of divorce (although without attempting to dodge this aspect of the biblical text) and embraced a wider audience that included, significantly, the preacher himself. That is to say, the process of bisociation, of playing with fire, enabled me in this particular case to face myself more squarely. In goading the gospel text by means of the Ukrainian harvest narrative I discovered what for me was a more self-involving, perhaps even self-involved, sermon, despite having numbered myself among those for whom the topic of divorce could easily have been off-putting.

From Myth to Parable

Natural typecasting led me to assign the Zeneca corporation to the role of the Pharisees in this sermon, given that each of these noxious players seemed only to ask what it could do, not what it should do, in relation to others and thereby wreaked havoc throughout its respective narrative. Typecasting alone, however, rarely makes for compelling sermons, since it tends to allow preacher and congregation alike to distance themselves from the antagonists of the stories; because we are neither Zeneca nor Pharisees, we convince ourselves, Jesus' reprimands are of no concern to us.

How, then, does one sufficiently destabilize this story so as to break it open just enough to encompass oneself? Put differently, how might one jolt this text or find it to have been jolted from its entrenchment as myth to a subversiveness as parable, according to the distinction drawn by Frank Kermode, a literary critic, who said that "myths are the agents of stability, fictions the agents of change"?[15] John Dominic Crossan elaborates:

> Parables are fictions, not myths; they are meant to change, not reassure us. Parable is always a somewhat unnerving experience. You can usually recognize a parable because your immediate reaction will be self-contradictory: "I don't know what you mean by that story but I'm certain I don't like it." To be human and to remain open to transcendental experience demands a willingness to be "parabled."[16]

He continues,

> The surface function of parable is to create contradiction within a given situation of complacent security but, even more unnervingly, to challenge the fundamental principle [of myth, which is that all contradictions can be reconciled] by making us aware of the fact that *we made*

up the reconciliation…You have built a lovely home, myth assures us; but, whispers parable, you are right above an earthquake fault.[17]

Parable, then, according to Crossan, "is story grown self-conscious and self-critical."

The more pressing question for me in discovering this sermon, then, became the self-conscious and self-critical one of how to see these texts less as complacent myths that confirmed what I already knew and believed and more as predatory parables that threatened to undo that same knowledge and belief. The question became one of wondering whether the preacher himself at times played the very role of the Pharisees, perhaps in relation to matters of divorce but with regard to other more personally urgent concerns of mine as well. In what circumstances, I wondered, might I, too, ask less what I should do than what I could do, and how might this tendency impinge on my own significant relationships?

In the biblical text, Mark depicts Jesus as resolute on the question of divorce, to be sure, but portrays him in this instance as even more adamantly opposed to the insinuations of the Pharisees. Preachers and parishioners fortunate to find themselves above the fray on issues of divorce are not likely to fare so well in terms of what Jesus perceives here as a rancor of the heart. While Jesus was not likely to stop loving the divorced, I figured, he must have been tempted to stop loving these Pharisees, even as at times in my own life I fear that he must have difficulty continuing to love me. The divorced, the Pharisees, and the preacher may thus share far more in common in terms of their poignant insecurity than one might at first assume. I, too, may know something of what it means to try to "get one over" on God and on intimate others when they, for their parts, would rather only that I enjoy their authentic love. In the present sermon then, this self-conscious attempt to turn to the subversive occurs in my saying, "Rather, I think, we should be grateful for divorced persons in our midst, for they know far better than most what it is to live not by works, by what they can get away with, but by the grace of God, who rescued them in the painful separations and losses of love and life."

This usual tendency to identify with the antagonist in my preaching became complicated in this instance, however, in that in contemplating the story of the Ukrainian harvest I suddenly remembered what struck me as a relevant moment from my own past—the BIC razor incident—in which I found myself cast in the less familiar role of the hero. I was the one who, in this story, somehow managed to get things right, whereas the woman who cut my hair and tourists who on previous occasions must have given my Soviet guide the inferior goods got things wrong. I wondered, *Can I allow myself to be a minor hero in one story of this sermon while identifying with the major villains in its other stories?* More important, should a preacher ever play the protagonist, in essence presuming to take on God's role in the narrative?

In this case, my answer to these questions was an unqualified yes. I was glad to have remembered this story, one both too telling and too comical to have passed by. This became still another of those moments of having sensed that I had no choice but to listen to my life, to let the material talk back while writing a sermon, despite here having to depict myself as being uncharacteristically in the right. I allowed my rule of entertaining what is of interest to the preacher to take precedence over my other rule of consistency of roles across narratives. In this sermon, I would play two parts, both God and the devil, so to speak, an act of creativity, however modest, as well as of abomination. Whether this choice became the exception that proves the rule, that proves only the exception, or that proves nothing at all I leave finally for the reader to decide.

Blessing the Children

An esteemed preacher, father of a then thirteen-year-old son, once told me that he tried to speak to young people his son's age in his sermons. Over lunch following the Sunday worship service he would ask the boy what he had taken from the sermon, and on those occasions when his son could articulate something of the sermon's essence as the father also understood it, the preacher felt that he had gauged the sermon appropriately. I took this minister's wisdom to heart and have since consciously attempted to consider the needs of young people in my own preaching, including children who have not yet reached adolescence.

Attending to the needs of children and youth in one's sermons does not mean having to talk down to the adults in the congregation but usually does involve the preacher's striving for ruthless uniformity of theme, for concrete words and imagery, and, whenever possible, for stories of interest to the preacher that may also be relevant to young people. Tilting sermons in this direction is not as difficult as it may at first seem, if in the process of discovering a sermon the preacher personally attends to the desires and concerns of the ordinarily silent, even preverbal, child within.

There were no children present in the congregation when I preached the sermon of this chapter. Even so, were I to preach on this same text to that same seminary community today, I would be more inclined to emphasize what previously seemed a bothersome peculiarity at best, namely, the fact that the lectionary passage ended not with Jesus' teaching on divorce but with his blessing the children. *Why,* I wondered, *did the lectionary not conclude with the disciples asking Jesus to clarify the controversy surrounding divorce? How did those children manage to sneak in? Did those who devised the lectionary reading sense a relationship between how adults relate to one another and the fate of children? Was there something more going on here than Mark's own suggestion, in his juxtaposing of the two episodes, that Jesus preferred the joyful prattle of children over the hard, insinuating voices of adults?*

As it stands, the sermon does include passing references to Jesus' blessing the children ("There was enough of him even for them, room at the table even for them," among others) without compromising, I think, and more likely reinforcing, the sermon's central theme of the abundance of what God desires for God's people. Even without the presence of children in that congregation, however, I now wish that I would have attempted to link the two narratives more integrally, given that the preacher and each person present were themselves once children, trusting and full of promise, and that each in turn had subsequently become, if not through divorce then by some other means, wounded and worried over having lost their favor with God. I think of a poem by William Stafford entitled, simply, "Scars":

They tell how it was, and how time
came along, and how it happened
again and again. They tell
the slant life takes when it turns
and slashes your face as a friend.

Any wound is real. In church
a woman lets the sun find
her cheek, and we see the lesson:
there are years in that book; there are sorrows
a choir can't reach when they sing.

Rows of children lift their faces of promise,
places where the scars will be.[18]

Quoting his Benedictine colleague Dom Sebastian Moore, psychologist of religion John McDargh suggests that the "primary and irreducible proposition about human beings…is that 'we all desire to be desired by the one we desire.'" Moore writes, "The only serious form of the religious question today is: Is human awareness, when it finds its fulfillment in love, resonating, albeit faintly, with an origin that 'behaves,' infinitely and all-constitutingly, as love behaves?" McDargh continues, "To ask this question in the poetry of the biblical tradition, 'Does God have regard for me?' or 'Am I source of delight to the Source of my delight?'"[19]

And he took them up in his arms, laid his hands on them, and blessed them.

Epilogue

Near the end of his commencement address to the Harvard Divinity School in 1838, Ralph Waldo Emerson pondered with the young ministers how they might respond in the face of the "smouldering, nigh quenched fires on the altar" and "manifest evils" of the church. One not usually thought to have championed conventional social or religious institutions, Emerson there called the graduates to a suspicion not of traditional but of innovative religious rites and cultural forms of his day. With words that now seem prescient in the aftermath of the ravages of history that would follow, he said, "I confess, all attempts to project and establish a Cultus with new rites and forms seem to me vain. Faith makes us, and not we it, and faith makes its own forms. All attempts to contrive a system are as cold as the new worship introduced by the French to the goddess of Reason—today, pasteboard and filigree and ending tomorrow in madness and murder."[1] In contrast to caricatures of Emerson as one opposed to any communal claims on the individual, in the Divinity School address he encouraged his hearers to breathe new life into existing institutions and forms of faith, "for, if once you are alive, you shall find [that these forms] shall become plastic and new. The remedy to their deformity is, first, soul, and second, soul, and evermore, soul."[2]

What traditional religious forms did Emerson have in mind? What "inestimable advantages" did he believe Christianity had conferred on the world that, when refreshed by the minister's own soul, would continue to "uplift and vivify" others? First, he said, was "the Sabbath, the jubilee of the whole world; whose light dawns welcome alike into the closet of the philosopher, into the garret of toil, and into prison cells, and everywhere suggests, even to the vile, the dignity of the spiritual being." The second, significantly, was "the institution of preaching—the speech of man to men—essentially the most flexible of all organs, of all forms." "What hinders [you] now," Emerson asked the ministers rhetorically, "everywhere, in pulpits, in lecture-rooms, in houses, in fields, wherever the invitation of men or your own occasions lead you, [from speaking] the very truth, as your life and conscience teach it, and [from] cheer[ing] the waiting, fainting hearts of men with new hope and new revelation?"[3]

I, too, would echo Emerson's convictions concerning the power for healing and hope somehow inherent in Sabbath rest and Christian preaching, but also, with him, would plead for ministers in our day to infuse these historic forms anew with soul, soul, and soul. As one on any given Sunday more likely to be found sitting in a pew than standing in a pulpit, I, too, with Emerson, cling to a desire for liberation "from the need to be finished" that the Sabbath affords,[4] while yearning within that unnatural interruption in time for a word—above all else, I think, for a direct, honest word—from the preacher's own depths, the preacher's own soul.

This capacity to tell the truth, I have attempted to argue, derives far more from the preacher's intensity of attention, the preacher's love, than from her eloquence of expression; far more from the preacher's finding himself bereft of words than awash in them; far more from childlike, even childish, playfulness than from mature earnestness; far more from acknowledging hidden, even unspeakable, desires, if only to oneself, than from seeking to contain or conceal them, especially from oneself; far more from pressing the limits than from coloring within the lines. As the angels hinted to the disciples in the aftermath of Jesus' ascension, we are likely to find the One for whom we long less in the clouds of spiritual heights than far down the mountain in the stench of soulful depths—in the mundane particularities, the fierce complexities, the simple pleasures of everyday life. There, as little children continue to bear witness, truth is both created and found. There, in our capacity to be alone, souls are both created and found. There, in the mysteries of our silence, salvation is both created and found. There, in the terrors of our boredom, the Saboteur of foregone conclusions, the Source of our delight, is both created and found.

Preaching to Death

The sermon that follows brings us full circle to consider, here at the end, what was for me the unsettling image with which this book began, that of little children walking beyond the graveyard surrounding the church where I worship. It strikes me in hindsight that the juxtaposition of those children and that graveyard has quietly infiltrated the whole of the book—in my urging ministers to reclaim their childlike heritage of play and desire, and in my arguing that certain social and ecclesial pressures inevitably diminish or deaden that capacity for play and desire. Indeed, even appropriate playfulness leads the preacher into increasingly threatening social venues (playing with strangers) and risky theological complexities (playing with fire), themselves fraught with death.

But perhaps that is the point: that play, and especially the play of preaching, is always caught up with death. We play at preaching because of, and in the face of, death. Emerson, at least, made his bold claims for the healing power of preaching as one familiar with the incalculable losses of death. His father, for one, had died when Emerson was still a young boy. More raw for him than this, however, was the loss of his wife, Ellen, who, barely twenty, had died of tuberculosis just seven years before the Divinity School address. Married less than two years and desolate with grief, his life and faith unraveling, Emerson would walk every day to her grave. On one such visit in March of 1832, fourteen months after her death, he walked into the family tomb and stared death in the face; he opened Ellen's coffin. "The act," writes a biographer, "was essential Emerson. He had to see for himself. Some part of him was not able to believe she was dead. Perhaps the very deadness of the body would help a belief in the life of the spirit."[5] "We return with an eagerness to the tomb," Emerson wrote, "as the only place of healing and peace."[6] Then, in 1842, less than four years after the Divinity School address, Emerson's son Waldo, his firstborn, died from scarlet fever at the age of five. Three days later Emerson wrote in his journal, "Sorrow makes us all children again, destroys all differences of intellect. The wisest knows nothing."[7] Death makes us children, and for our sakes, for us who mourn, is the foolishness and play of preaching.

A Concluding Benediction

I preached the book's final sermon, "Children of the Resurrection," to members and ministers of that church in the midst of a graveyard, which I mentioned in the Introduction, where ordinarily I listen to sermons of others. The occasion for the sermon, based on the lectionary gospel text of the day, was the culmination of the annual stewardship campaign of this generally affluent, suburban parish on a special Sunday in November. The congregation, I felt, would readily be able to identify with the image of the children and graveyard that had earlier caught my eye just outside those windows. I offer that image, then, and the sermon I discovered therein as a conclusion to this book and as a benediction of sorts to my readers.

Some Sadducees, those who say there is no resurrection, came to [Jesus] and asked him a question, "Teacher, Moses wrote for us that if a man's brother dies, leaving a wife but no children, the man shall marry the widow and raise up children for his brother. Now there were seven brothers; the first married, and died childless; then the second and the third [brothers] married her, and so in the same way all seven died childless. Finally the woman also died. In the resurrection, therefore, whose wife will the woman be? For the seven had married her."

Jesus said to them, "Those who belong to this age marry and are given in marriage; but those who are considered worthy of a place in that age and in the resurrection from the dead neither marry nor are given in marriage. Indeed they cannot die anymore, because they are like angels and are children of God, being children of the resurrection. And the fact that the dead are raised Moses himself showed, in the story about the bush, where he speaks of the Lord as the God of Abraham, the God of Isaac, and the God of Jacob. Now he is God not of the dead, but of the living; for to him all of them are alive." (Lk. 20:27–38)

■ Children of the Resurrection ■

She was no stranger to death; she had known her share of death for her thirteen short years. Not big deaths, mind you, probably not actual death, but little deaths, to be sure, the kind almost all of us die, though some more than others, in one small way or another most every day—the deaths that chisel away, ever so slowly, at our hearts and souls, the deaths that rob us of vitality and joy and life. Death was something she could get her hands around; death she knew.

"Watching classmates strut past in designer clothes," Dirk Johnson wrote recently in *The New York Times,* "Wendy Williams sat silently on the yellow school bus, wearing a cheap belt and rummage-sale slacks. One boy stopped and yanked his thumb, demanding her seat. 'Move it, trailer girl', he sneered."

Small deaths like that. You know the kind I'm talking about.

Wendy lives in a tin trailer home in a trailer park euphemistically named Chateau Estates in Ronald Reagan's hometown of Dixon, Illinois, but she attends Reagan Middle School with young people from homes worth hundreds of thousands of dollars, not unlike those sprouting from cornfields around this church. Her classmates play on thousand-dollar computers, vacation at Disney World, wear the coveted Tommy Hilfiger label on their clothes. But not Wendy.

"I told this girl: 'That's a really awesome shirt. Where did you get it?'" said Wendy, explaining that she knew it was out of her price range, but that she wanted to join the small talk. "And she looked at me and laughed and said, 'Why would you want to know?'"

Wendy tries to hide a slight overbite by pursing her lips, a humiliation not lost on her classmates who mock her with the nickname Rabbit, one that she begged her parents "to avoid by sending her to an orthodontist," which they cannot afford.

"'Do you know what it's like?' asked Wendy's mother, Veronica Williams, 'to have your daughter come home and say,

"Mom, the kids say my clothes are tacky," and then walk off with her head hanging low?"[8] Her mother, it seems, knows something of little deaths, too, which I mentioned in the Introduction.

■

So you can't really blame the Sadducees for getting a bit caught up with death, for obsessing a little, for concluding that there seems to be a lot of that sort of thing going around these days, death bordering on epidemic, not a few of which they couldn't have helped but die already themselves—little deaths like yours and mine and Wendy Williams' and her mother's. There's plenty of evidence to back up the Sadducees' claims that death is pretty much all she wrote, that there's not much sense in getting all worked up over an afterlife, that what you see is what you get, and that what you see, more often than not, is one or another bully on the bus yanking his thumb and telling trailer girls to move it, and what you get is some Tommy Hilfiger girl in the hall scornfully wondering why we'd like to know. Death is all around us and in us, you and me. We know what those Sadducees are talking about; we've felt it, we've died it, ourselves.

Some Sadducees, those who say there is no resurrection, came to [Jesus] and asked him a question. And who of us hasn't had a question or two about resurrection to put to Jesus right along with them, what with death all around?

■

Several months ago as I was sitting during worship on my uncomfortable pew in this very sanctuary, I happened to glance out the window shortly after the young children had been dismissed to go to their Young Church activity in the other building and saw the children walking in the distance beyond the cemetery. I had witnessed a similar scene, of course, as you have, on many previous occasions. This time, however, something about those children walking past that graveyard on their way to class captured my attention, as if I were at last seeing them for the first time. Something in me momentarily recoiled at seeing those children so near to those dead. Children and death, some voice in me protested, should not walk so closely to one another, though the children themselves didn't seem to mind. Yet the easy proximity of those unassuming young lives to the shadow of death unsettled me for a moment before my thoughts returned inside to the minister reading the morning scripture lesson.

But let's not kid ourselves. Most of us need only think back for a moment to our own childhoods to know how many times even such fragile lives as these have already come to taste death, have experienced, at the very least, those little deaths that rob us slowly of vitality and joy and life, those little deaths on the playground or in the classroom or at home, death by fear or loneliness or ridicule or rejection. I would even wager that most graphic among what we remember from childhood is precisely such moments of our little deaths, our humiliations, our griefs. What child among us doesn't know, what child within us doesn't remember, something of that graveyard at least, even without walking past the tombstones every Sunday? How many ways they have died already, how many, you and I. Death is something we Sadducees can get our hands around; death we know. But resurrection? Life?

■

So it shouldn't come as much of a surprise to us that the test question they choose to stump the rabbi is one that emerges from their realm of expertise, a test question reeking of death, of unimaginable grief, of unspeakable pain and horror:

Teacher, Moses wrote for us that if a man's brother dies, leaving a wife but no children, the man shall marry the widow and raise up children for his brother. Now [suppose] there were seven brothers; the first married, and died childless; then the second and the third married her, and so in the same way all seven died childless. Finally the woman also died. In the resurrection, therefore, whose wife will the woman be? For the seven had married her.

The Sadducees of their day were not unlike the leadership of some Christian coalitions of ours, the aristocratic arch-conservatives with considerable religious influence and no small appetite for secular political power. The Sadducees saturated the airwaves with their saccharine certitude. They knew the law well enough, they'd written the book on virtues, and, in fact, their Bible consisted only of books of the Law, only the books of Moses, the Torah—only Genesis, Exodus, Leviticus, Numbers, and Deuteronomy. They'd rejected the rest of the Hebrew Scriptures as too left of center, and so far as they could tell in these, their favorite five books, there wasn't so much as a peep about any resurrection from the dead. There's plenty of death in the Torah, to be sure; death they seemed able to find there and accept, but not much hint of resurrection, not much to go on by way of life.

So they choose one of Moses' statutes concerning marriage—one from Genesis 8 and Deuteronomy 25—that instructs a man to marry his brother's widow if his brother dies childless, a law seeking to protect the widow and to keep property in the family by raising up a child, an heir, to inherit it. And then the Sadducees proceed to play this statute out to tragic absurdity. They say, suppose there were seven brothers, and one after another they marry their brother's widow but all die in succession childless, even finally the much-to-be-pitied widow of the whole sordid lot. Moses, they tell Jesus, couldn't have believed in a resurrection if he'd set down a statute such as this, for *in the resurrection whose wife will the woman be? For the seven had married her.* Whose is she now, they wanted Jesus to tell them. To whom does she belong now?

Death was something those Sadducees could get their hands around; death they knew. And so do we.

■

Woody Wassan, the principal at Wendy's middle school, tries to ask his students about their dreams and aspirations: "They want to be doctors, lawyers, veterinarians and, of course, professional athletes," said Mr. Wasson. "I don't remember the last time I heard somebody say they wanted to be a police officer or a firefighter. They want to do something that will make a lot of money and have a lot of prestige."

"'Wendy goes to school around these rich kids,' her mother said, 'and wonders why she can't have things like they do.' A bright girl with a flair for art, writing, and numbers, Wendy stays up late most nights reading books." But she declined a recent invitation from one of her teachers to join an accelerated algebra class: "'I get picked on for my clothes and living in the trailer park,' said Wendy, who never brings anyone home from school. 'I don't want to get picked on for being a nerd, too.'"

Death we can get our hands around; death we know. But resurrection? Life?

Jesus said to them, "Those who belong to this age marry and are given in marriage; but those who are considered worthy of a place in that age and in the resurrection from the dead neither marry nor are given in marriage. Indeed they cannot die anymore, because they are like angels and are children of God, being children of the resurrection. And the fact that the dead are raised Moses himself showed, in the story of the bush, where he speaks of the Lord as the God of Abraham, the God of Isaac, and the God of Jacob. Now he is God not of the dead, but of the living; for to him all of them are alive."

It's a good thing that I'm telling you Luke's version of this story instead of the one in the gospel of Mark, chapter 12, for if I were telling you Mark's version, you'd learn that Jesus' initial response to the Sadducees was not nearly so polite as in Luke. You'd have to find out that in Mark, Jesus starts out by telling the Sadducees that they're dead wrong in that they know nothing of the scriptures nor of the power of God. "You Bible-bangers," he tells them there in Mark, "know neither your Bibles nor the 'bang' of God." Fortunately, however, Luke spares me from having to point out such unpleasantries.

Even the Moses of the Torah, the Sadducees' Bible, Jesus goes on to say, must have known there was a resurrection, for when God spoke to Moses from the burning bush God said, "I *am* the God of Abraham, I *am* the God of Isaac, I *am* the God of Jacob,"—I *am,* present tense, not I *was,* past tense—"the God of these your forebears, who by the time of Moses were long since dead. Yes, of course they have died, but I *am* their God," Moses hears burning from that bush. "I know them intimately still, I know them by name, I know them," God says. "I know them, I am with them, and they are with me. I keep my promise to them," says God. Even Moses must have known, Jesus tells them, that God is God not of the dead, but of the living; for to him all of them are alive.

If only you knew, Jesus tells us, you who know death by heart, if only you could comprehend or even imagine a life without fear or grief or shame, a place where death has died and where none can die anymore, because they are like angels, because you are equal to angels and are children of God, being children of the resurrection.

"If only you knew," Jesus cries out, "you wouldn't ask, Whose wife will the woman be? Whose is she now, whose is she now, to whom does she belong now? You wouldn't ask, because you would know she is God's, she is God's, she is free, she belongs to God! In life and in death we belong to God!

■

Wendy went to a guidance counselor, Cynthia Kowa Basler, a dynamic woman who keeps close tabs on the children, especially girls who fret about their weight and suddenly stop eating.

"I feel a little down," Wendy told her. So the counselor gathered eight students, including other girls like Wendy, who felt embarrassed about their economic station.

In this school named for Ronald Reagan, the students were told to study the words of Eleanor Roosevelt. One of her famous quotations was posted above the counselor's desk: "No one can make you feel inferior without your consent."

As a group, the students looked up the definitions of inferior and consent.

And then they read the words out loud.
"Again," the counselor instructed.
"Louder," the counselor insisted.

Again and again, they read the inspirational words.

Life still has plenty of bumps. When Wendy gets off the school bus—the trailer park is the first stop, so everyone can see where she lives—she still looks at her shoes.

But her mother has noticed her smiling more these days. And Wendy has even said she might consider taking an advanced course in math, her favorite subject.

"I want to go to college," Wendy said the other day. "I want to become a teacher."

"She's going to make it," the counselor said, with a clenched fist and voice full of hope.

We bring our children to these uncomfortable pews in the middle of a graveyard Sunday after Sunday. We deliver them right smack into the shadow of death, which has either got to be an act of diabolical cruelty, of perverse morbidity bordering on child abuse (bringing children to a graveyard week after week?), *or* an act of severe mercy and audacious hope.

How can we know? How can we be sure? Are they, are you and I, children only of this age, children of death? Or are we children of God, children of the resurrection?

Beloved, this is not an academic question. For Jesus, at least, it was not merely a good afternoon's debate with the Sadducees, not simply a matter of arguing the Bible, of toying with Hebrew verb tenses—I *am,* I *was* the God—not merely intellectual prowess and wordplay. For Jesus, it meant more even than bolstering self-esteem, as important as these things may be. For Jesus, there was so much more at stake than this.

What was at stake, of course, was his life—his life, finally, at stake on a cross. There he is, dying, another much-to-be-pitied one of our whole sordid lot. Death is something Jesus can get his hands around. Those nails in the cross he can get his hands around. Death God knows.

But resurrection? Life?

■

One of my seminary teachers tells the story of one of his seminary teachers, Edmund Steimle, the noted Lutheran preacher and professor of homiletics of a previous generation at Union Seminary in New York. Steimle lost his wife of many years, Rosalind, on a Saturday before Easter:

> She got sick suddenly in the morning, sicker in the afternoon, and by nightfall she was gone. Steimle said, "I found myself the next day seated in the pew of my church on Easter Sunday, a church full of Easter lilies and a brass choir and a springtime congregation singing the 'Alleluia's,' and they stuck in my throat. I couldn't sing them, I did not believe in the resurrection, not that day, not with what had happened to me. I put down the hymn book. But as I listened to the congregation sing, I realized, "I don't have to believe in the resurrection today. They are believing in the resurrection for me until I can believe in it again for myself."[9]

■

Dear friends, you who know death by heart: Can you imagine a life without fear or grief or shame, a place where in Christ death has died and where none can die anymore? Can you imagine? Will you believe with me, will you help me believe against all odds that in Jesus Christ you and I are like angels and are children of God, children of the resurrection? That the God we dare to worship in the middle of this graveyard is the God not of the dead, but of the living, for to God all are alive? Can we help one another trust in this sacred time and place that in life and in death we belong to God?

Notes

Introduction

[1]W. H. Auden, *The English Auden: Poems, Essays, and Dramatic Writings, 1927–1939,* ed. Edward Mendelson (New York: Random House, 1977), 319.

[2]O. K. Bouwsma, *Wittgenstein: Conversations 1949–51* (Indianapolis: Hackett, 1986), quoted in Adam Phillips, *The Beast in the Nursery: On Curiosity and Other Appetites* (New York: Pantheon Books, 1998), 86.

[3]Ibid., 21.

[4]Frederick Buechner, *Telling Secrets: A Memoir* (San Francisco: Harper San Francisco, 1991), 36. Cf. James E. Dittes, *Minister on the Spot* (Philadelphia: Pilgrim Press, 1970), 84–85. Dittes suggests that many ministers acknowledge and lament as a form of bondage their personal and pastoral inhibitions; others, however, deny this tendency by trying "to make a virtue…out of [their] cool aloofness and non-involvement," pretentiously criticizing other ministers involved in any particular ministry.

[5]Phillips, *The Beast in the Nursery,* 35.

[6]Jürgen Moltmann, *The Future of Creation: Collected Essays,* trans. Margaret Kohl (Philadelphia: Fortress Press, 1979), 143.

[7]Cf. J. Randall Nichols, *The Restoring Word: Preaching as Pastoral Communication* (San Francisco: Harper & Row, 1987), 14–22. Pastoral preaching is, for Nichols, "the homiletical occasion when, whether by its dimension, its strategy, or its subject, a sermon addresses or impacts the personally invested concerns of its hearers," but then, more candidly, "as much as anything a posture, a sensitivity, an attitude" gleaned in large measure from influential mentors who shape and guide the preacher (18).

[8]D. W. Winnicott, "The Capacity to be Alone," chap. 2 of *The Maturational Processes and the Facilitating Environment: Studies in the Theory of Emotional Development* (Madison, Conn: International Universities Press, 1965), 29–36.

[9]Sara Rimer, "A Shy Scholar Transforms Dartmouth Into a Haven for Intellectuals," *New York Times,* 4 January 1997, 6A.

[10]Ralph Waldo Emerson, *The Heart of Emerson's Journals,* ed. Bliss Perry (New York: Dover Publications, 1958), 39.

[11]The Episcopal Church, *The Book of Common Prayer* (New York: The Seabury Press, 1979), 323.

Chapter 1: Playing with the Text

[1]M. Masud R. Khan's "Introduction," in Winnicott, *Holding and Interpretation: Fragment of an Analysis* (New York: Grove Press, 1972, 1986), 1. Heinz Kohut, an influential American psychoanalyst, expressed similar sentiments in *The Analysis of the Self: A Systematic Approach to the Psychoanalytic Treatment of Narcissistic Personality Disorders,* monograph no. 4 of *The Psychoanalytic Study of the Child,* ed. Ruth S. Eissler et al. (New York: International Universities Press, 1971), 273: "The most common dangers to which the analyst is exposed [in treating pathological narcissists] are boredom, lack of emotional involvement with the patient, and precarious maintenance of attention."

[2]Khan, in Winnicott, *Holding and Interpretation,* esp. pp. 1–7.

[3]See Phillips, *Winnicott* (Cambridge: Harvard University Press, 1988), esp. pp. 22–38; and James W. Jones, "Playing and Believing: The Uses of D. W. Winnicott in the Psychology of Religion," in Janet Liebman Jacobs and Donald Capps, eds., *Religion, Society, and Psychoanalysis: Readings in Contemporary Theory* (Boulder: Westview Press, 1997), 106–26, esp. pp. 107–10. See also Brett Kahr, *D. W. Winnicott: A Biographical Portrait* (Madison, Conn.: International Universities Press, 1996).

[4]Winnicott, "The Observation of Infants in a Set Situation," in *Through Paediatrics to Psychoanalysis* (London: Hogarth Press, 1975), 52–53, 66; see also Phillips, "On Being Bored," chap. 7 of *On Kissing, Tickling, and Being Bored: Psychoanalytic Essays on the Unexamined Life* (Cambridge: Harvard University Press, 1993), 68–78, esp. 72–74.

[5]Winnicott, *Through Paediatrics to Psychoanalysis,* 53–54.

[6]See "The Concept of a Healthy Individual," in Winnicott, *Home Is Where We Start From: Essays by a Psychoanalyst* (New York: W. W. Norton, 1986), 22, 27–28; and Jay R. Greenberg and Stephen A. Mitchell, *Object Relations in Psychoanalytic Theory* (Cambridge: Harvard University Press, 1983), 191, 201.

[7]Phillips, *Winnicott,* 138, 140. He is quoting from "Child Analysis in the Latency Period" (1958), chap. 10 in Winnicott, *The Maturational Processes and the Facilitating Environment: Studies in the Theory of Emotional Development* (Madison, Conn.: International Universities Press, 1958), 122.

[8]Jones, in Jacobs and Capps, eds., *Religion, Society, and Psychoanalysis,* 117, quoting from G. Lakoff and M. Johnson, *Metaphors We Live By* (Chicago: University of Chicago Press, 1980), 230. See also Winnicott, *Home is Where We Start From,* 30; and idem, *The Maturational Processes and the Facilitating Environment,* 181.

[9]See, e.g., Thomas G. Long, *The Witness of Preaching* (Louisville: Westminster/ John Knox Press, 1989), 62–63.

[10]Winnicott, *Playing and Reality* (New York: Routledge, 1992), 4.

[11]Ibid., 3.

[12]Ibid., 5.

[13]See, e.g., ibid., 10–11; and idem, *The Maturational Processes and the Facilitating Environment,* 181.

[14]Phillips, *Winnicott,* 101.

[15]Winnicott, "The Capacity to be Alone," 29, 31.

[16]Greenberg and Mitchell, *Object Relations in Psychoanalytic Theory,* 190.

[17]Capps, *Agents of Hope: A Pastoral Psychology* (Minneapolis: Fortress Press, 1995), 51.

[18]Winnicott, "The Capacity to be Alone," 30, emphasis in original.

[19]Ibid., 34.

[20]Phillips, *On Kissing, Tickling, and Being Bored,* 69. Donald Capps in *Agents of Hope,* 51, further clarifies Winnicott's connection between solitude, the benign presence of the other, and hope: "What does solitariness have to do with hoping? [I]t is vital to hoping, because it means that we have internalized the object of our desire, that it is 'out there' and 'in here' at one and the same time. Without such internalization, we would be consumed by anxiety as we await the one who is to come. With it, we have a stable attitude of hope, for the one for whom we wait is, paradoxically, already here." Hope, for Capps, is based on the felt sense that one is not alone, even *when* alone.

[21]Phillips, *On Kissing, Tickling, and Being Bored,* 69, 70.

[22]Winnicott, "Anxiety Associated with Insecurity" (1952), quoted in Kahn's introduction to Winnicott, *Holding and Interpretation,* 5.

[23]Kahn, in Winnicott, *Holding and Interpretation,* 2–3.

[24]Phillips, "On Risk and Solitude," in *On Kissing, Tickling, and Being Bored,* 33–34.

[25]Dittes, *Minister on the Spot* (Philadelphia: Pilgrim Press, 1970), 84–85.

[26]Capps, *Men, Religion, and Melancholia: James, Otto, Jung, and Erikson* (New Haven: Yale University Press, 1997), 3–4.

[27]Douglas Coupland, *Life After God* (New York: Simon & Schuster, 1995), 271–72.

[28]Ibid., 273.

[29]Ibid., 309, 313, 359.

[30]Gary Dorrien, *The Word as True Myth: Interpreting Modern Theology* (Louisville: Westminster John Knox Press, 1997), 224–25.

[31]Cf. Robert C. Dykstra, *Counseling Troubled Youth* (Louisville: Westminster John Knox Press, 1997), 83–89.

Chapter 2: Playing Witness to Life

[1]Ian Pitt-Watson, *Preaching: A Kind of Folly* (Philadelphia: Westminster Press, 1976), 68–72.

[2]Saint Augustine, *Enarrationes in Psalmos,* viii, 13, quoted in John T. McNeill and Helena M. Gamer, *Medieval Handbooks of Penance* (New York: Octagon Books, 1965), 18–19.

[3]Augustine, *Confessions,* 8:12, trans. R. S. Pine-Coffin (Harmondsworth, England: Penguin Books, 1979), 177.

[4]Anne Hunsaker Hawkins, "St. Augustine: Archetypes of Family," in *The Hunger of the Heart: Reflections on the 'Confessions' of Augustine,* monograph 8, ed. Donald Capps and James E. Dittes (West Lafayette, Ind.: Society for the Scientific Study of Religion, 1990), 240, argues that "hunger is itself a chief metaphor in the *Confessions*—a metaphor that relates the restlessness of body, mind, and heart alike to the archetypal mother, source of nourishment and cause of both satisfaction and frustration."

[5]Adam Phillips, *The Beast in the Nursery: On Curiosity and Other Appetites* (New York: Pantheon Books, 1998), xx–xxi.

[6]Ibid., 3–4, 7, 65.

[7]Ibid., 11, 18.

[8]Ibid., 21.

[9]Ibid., 21–22, 24. Phillips notes here the irony in Freud's own apparent need for followers who would adhere faithfully to his theories. Similarly problematic, we might add, is the compliance inherent in affirming Winnicott's negative evaluation of compliance.

[10]Ibid., 22–23; 157–58, n. 2.

[11]Dittes, *Minister on the Spot* (Philadelphia: Pilgrim Press, 1970), 87–88.

[12]Phillips, *The Beast in the Nursery,* 150.

[13]Ibid., 48, 29.

[14]Sigmund Freud, "On the Sexual Theories of Children," quoted in Phillips, *The Beast in the Nursery,* 73.

[15]Augustine, *Confessions,* 2:3.

[16]Phillips, *The Beast in the Nursery,* 52–53.

[17]D. W. Winnicott, "Yes, But How Do We Know It's True?" in *Thinking About Children,* ed. Ray Shepherd, Jennifer Johns, and Helen Taylor Robinson (Reading, Mass.: Addison-Wesley Publishing, 1996), 13–14; cf. Phillips, *The Beast in the Nursery,* 65–66.

[18]Winnicott, *Playing and Reality* (New York: Routledge, 1992), 90, 145.

[19]Phillips, *The Beast in the Nursery,* 67.

[20]Ibid., 67–68.

[21]Ibid., xvii, 6.

[22]Ibid., 37.

[23]This sermon was published previously under the same title in *The Princeton Seminary Bulletin* 20/2 (July 1999): 183–88; and as "Unrealistic to the Core," in *The Christian Ministry* (September/October 1999): 14–17.

[24]Capps, *Life Cycle Theory and Pastoral Care* (Philadelphia: Fortress Press, 1983), 85–86, 91. Cf. Helen Merrell Lynd, *On Shame and the Search for Identity* (New York: Harcourt Brace, 1958), chap. 2.

[25]Capps, *Life Cycle Theory and Pastoral Care,* 92 (emphasis added).

[26]Ibid., 92. He is quoting Erik H. Erikson, *Young Man Luther* (New York: W. W. Norton, 1958), 213.

[27]Ibid., 94.

[28]Augustine, *Confessions,* 4:4.

[29]Ibid., 4:7. Cf. also, Capps, *Life Cycle Theory and Pastoral Care,* 90–92; and idem, "The Scourge of Shame and the Silencing of Adeodatus," in Capps and Dittes, eds., *The Hunger of the Heart,* 69–92, esp. pp. 77–79.

Chapter 3: Playing with Strangers

[1]Bertram D. Lewin, "Dream Psychology and the Analytic Situation," in Melvin R. Lansky, ed., *Essential Papers on Dreams* (New York: New York University Press, 1992), 62. Lewin cites Ernest Jones, *The Life and Work of Sigmund Freud,* vol. 1 (New York: Basic Books, 1953); and Gregory Zilboorg, "Some Sidelights on Free Associations," *International Journal of Psychoanalysis* 33 (1952): 489–95.

[2]T. M. Luhrmann, *Of Two Minds: The Growing Disorder in American Psychiatry* (New York: Alfred A. Knopf, 2000), 189–90.

[3]Ibid., 192.

[4]James E. Dittes, *Pastoral Counseling: The Basics* (Louisville: Westminster John Knox Press, 1999), 11.

[5]Like Dittes, Tanya Luhrmann finds in the professional self-restraint of psychoanalysts an analogy to divine love: "There is, in fact, a somewhat Christian feel to contemporary psychoanalysis, though most psychoanalysts might be taken aback by that characterization. Their love for patients is rarely stated in such bald terms as to make the comparison striking. Nonetheless, the love represented in the Christian tradition is not so dissimilar to the way that analysts conceive of their care for the patient. The psychoanalytic credo that self-knowledge and authenticity are good and help to make us good really must be framed within a belief that love will make us loving and that when we love we trust others and protect them…[Psychoanalysts] quickly qualify the kind of love they mean: not carnal, not possessive. They seem to mean the kind of belief in another's capacity for goodness sometimes captured by the word *agape*…, the love of God for humankind" (Luhrmann, *Of Two Minds,* 201).

[6]Dittes, *Pastoral Counseling,* 147.

[7]Julia Kristeva, *Strangers to Ourselves,* trans. Leon S. Roudiez (New York: Columbia University Press, 1991), 1.

[8]Jürgen Moltmann, *God in Creation: A New Theology of Creation and the Spirit of God,* trans. Margaret Kohl (San Francisco: Harper & Row, 1985), 86–88.

[9]Chapter 2 of Evelyn Fox Keller, *A Feeling for the Organism: The Life and Work of Barbara McClintock* (New York: W. H. Freeman, 1983), is entitled "The Capacity to Be Alone."

[10]Ibid., 97, xxi.

[11]Ibid., xxi.

[12]Ibid., 97.

[13]Ibid., 198.

[14]Ibid., 102.

[15]Ibid., 115–17.

[16]Ibid., 114.

[17]Ibid., 103.

[18]Ibid., 179.

[19]Gina Kolata, "Dr. Barbara McClintock, 90, Gene Research Pioneer, Dies," *New York Times,* 4 September 1992, 1A.

[20]See in this regard Donald Capps's discussion of the ultimately social trajectory of Emerson's individualism in "Expressive Individualism as Scapegoat," chap. 5 of Capps, *The Depleted Self: Sin in a Narcissistic Age* (Minneapolis: Fortress Press, 1993), esp. 109–11: "Emerson would not have devoted so much attention to the problem of social conformity, especially its destructive effects on one's inner character, if he did not assume that the individual would be an active participant in social life…Regaining one's selfhood is not achieved by escaping society or becoming antisocial." Rather, solitude serves as a corrective in those unfortunate but not uncommon cases where, in Emerson's words, "we let society choose for us, and if we miscarry in our first enterprises, we lose heart, and allow society to declare us ruined."

[21]Kristeva, *Strangers to Ourselves,* 3–4.

[22]Ibid., 3.

[23]Nina Coltart, *Slouching Towards Bethlehem* (New York: Guilford Press, 1992), 2.

[24]Adam Phillips, "Returning the Dream: In Memoriam Masud Khan," in *On Kissing, Tickling, and Being Bored: Psychoanalytic Essays on the Unexamined Life* (Cambridge: Harvard University Press, 1993), 59–67.

[25]Ibid., 62.

[26]Ibid., 64.

[27]Ibid., 65–66.

[28]Phillips, *On Flirtation: Psychoanalytic Essays on the Uncommitted Life* (Cambridge: Harvard University Press, 1994), 108.

[29]Phillips, *On Kissing, Tickling, and Being Bored,* 62.

[30]Ibid., 62–63.

[31]Ibid., 63.

[32]Phillips, *On Flirtation,* 108.

[33]From the PBS videotape *Facing Evil, with Bill Moyers,* KERA, Dallas-Fort Worth, Denton, and Public Affairs Television, 1988; Pacific Arts Video Publishing, 50 N. La Cienega Blvd., Beverly Hills, CA 90211.

Chapter 4: Playing with Fire

[1]Anne Fadiman, *The Spirit Catches You and You Fall Down: A Hmong Child, Her Doctors, and the Collision of Two Cultures* (New York: Farrar, Straus and Giroux, 1997), x.

[2]Carol Lakey Hess, "Abomination and Creativity: Shaking the Order of the Cosmos," *Princeton Seminary Bulletin* 15, no. 1 (1994): 28–43; cf. Arthur Koestler, *Insight and Outlook* (Lincoln: University of Nebraska Press, 1949), 317.

[3]Hess, "Abomination and Creativity," 39.

[4]Ibid., 28.

[5]Ibid., 36–37.

[6]Ibid., 43.

[7]Gardner C. Taylor, *How Shall They Preach: The Lyman Beecher Lectures and Five Lenten Sermons* (Elgin, Ill.: Progressive Baptist Publishing House, 1977), 58.

[8]Luther H. Martin, Huck Gutman, and Patrick H. Hutton, eds., *Technologies of the Self: A Seminar with Michel Foucault* (Amherst: University of Massachusetts Press, 1988), 9.

[9]William Stafford, *You Must Revise Your Life* (Ann Arbor: University of Michigan Press, 1986), ix.

[10]Ibid., 14–15.

[11]Ibid., 21.

[12]Ibid., 73.

[13]Omer Westendorf, "Finest Wheat," hymn text and music copyright of the Archdiocese of Philadelphia (1977), in *The Presbyterian Hymnal: Hymns, Psalms, and Spiritual Songs* (Louisville: Westminster John Knox Press, 1990), 521.

[14]Raymond Bonner with James Bennet, "A Bitter Harvest for Ukraine from an American Seed Deal," *New York Times,* 19 June 1994, 1A.

[15]Quoted in John Dominic Crossan, *The Dark Interval: Towards a Theology of Story* (Niles, Ill.: Argus Communications, 1975), 56.

[16]Ibid., 56.

[17]Ibid., 57 (emphasis in original).

[18]Stafford, *An Oregon Message* (New York: Harper & Row, 1987), 41.

[19]John McDargh, "Desire, Domination, and the Life and Death of the Soul," in *On Losing the Soul: Essays in the Social Psychology of Religion,* ed. Richard K. Fenn and Donald Capps (Albany: State University of New York Press, 1995), 226. See also Robert C. Dykstra, "Wedding of the Waters: Pastoral Theological Reflections on the Self," *International Journal of Practical Theology* 3/2 (1999): 251–68.

Epilogue

[1]Ralph Waldo Emerson, "The Divinity School Address," in Donald Capps and Richard K. Fenn, eds., *Individualism Reconsidered: Readings Bearing on the Endangered Self in Modern Society* (Princeton: Center for Religion, Self and Society, 1992), 149.

[2]Ibid., 149–50.

[3]Ibid., 150.

[4]Wayne Muller, *Sabbath: Restoring the Sacred Rhythm of Rest* (New York: Bantam Books, 1999), 83.

[5]Robert D. Richardson, Jr., *Emerson: The Mind on Fire* (Berkeley: University of California Press, 1995), 3.

[6]Susan L. Roberson, *Emerson in His Sermons: A Man-Made Self* (Columbia: University of Missouri Press, 1995), 94.

[7]Joel Porte, *Emerson in His Journals* (Cambridge: Harvard University Press, 1982), 277.

[8]Dirk Johnson, "When Money Is Everything, Except Hers," *New York Times,* 14 October 1998, 1A.

[9]Thomas G. Long, personal communication, Nov. 20, 1998.

Bibliography

Angelou, Maya. *I Know Why the Caged Bird Sings*. New York: Bantam Books, 1988.

Auden, W. H. *The English Auden: Poems, Essays, and Dramatic Writings, 1927–1939*. Edited by Edward Mendelson. New York: Random House, 1977.

Augustine. *Confessions*. Translated by R. S. Pine-Coffin. Harmondsworth, England: Penguin Books, 1979.

Bonner, Raymond, and James Bennet. "A Bitter Harvest for Ukraine from an American Seed Deal." *New York Times*, 19 June 1994, 1A.

Bouwsma, O. K. *Wittgenstein: Conversations 1949–51*. Indianapolis: Hackett, 1986.

Buechner, Frederick. *Telling Secrets: A Memoir*. San Francisco: HarperSan Francisco, 1991.

Capps, Donald. *Agents of Hope: A Pastoral Psychology*. Minneapolis: Fortress Press, 1995.

———. *The Depleted Self: Sin in a Narcissistic Age*. Minneapolis: Fortress Press, 1993.

———. *Life Cycle Theory and Pastoral Care*. Philadelphia: Fortress Press, 1983.

———. *Men, Religion, and Melancholia: James, Otto, Jung, and Erikson*. New Haven: Yale University Press, 1997.

———, and James E. Dittes, eds. *The Hunger of the Heart: Reflections on the 'Confessions' of Augustine*. West Lafayette, Ind.: Society for the Scientific Study of Religion, 1990.

———, and Richard K. Fenn, eds. *Individualism Reconsidered: Readings Bearing on the Endangered Self in Modern Society*, Monograph No. 1. Princeton: Center for Religion, Self and Society, 1992.

Coltart, Nina. *Slouching Towards Bethlehem*. New York: Guilford Press, 1992.

Coupland, Douglas. *Life After God*. New York: Simon & Schuster, 1995.

Crossan, John Dominic. *The Dark Interval: Towards a Theology of Story*. Niles, Ill.: Argus Communications, 1975.

Dittes, James E. *Minister on the Spot*. Philadelphia: Pilgrim Press, 1970.

————. *Pastoral Counseling: The Basics.* Louisville: Westminster John Knox Press, 1999.

Dorrien, Gary. *The Word as True Myth: Interpreting Modern Theology.* Louisville: Westminster John Knox Press, 1997.

Dykstra, Robert C. *Counseling Troubled Youth.* Louisville: Westminster John Knox Press, 1997.

————. "Unrealistic to the Core." *The Christian Ministry* (Sept./Oct. 1999): 14–17.

————. "The Unreality of God." *Princeton Seminary Bulletin* 20, no. 2 (July 1999): 183–88.

————. "Wedding of the Waters: Pastoral Theological Reflections on the Self." *International Journal of Practical Theology* 3, no. 2 (1999): 251–68.

Emerson, Ralph Waldo. The Divinity School Address. In *Individualism Reconsidered: Readings Bearing on the Endangered Self in Modern Society,* edited by Donald Capps and Richard K. Fenn, Monograph No. 1, 141–50. Princeton: Center for Religion, Self and Society, 1992.

————. *The Heart of Emerson's Journals.* Edited by Bliss Perry. New York: Dover Publications, 1958.

Episcopal Church. *The Book of Common Prayer.* New York: Seabury Press, 1979.

Erikson, Erik H. *Young Man Luther.* New York: W. W. Norton, 1958.

Fadiman, Anne. *The Spirit Catches You and You Fall Down: A Hmong Child, Her Doctors, and the Collision of Two Cultures.* New York: Farrar, Straus and Giroux, 1997.

Fenn, Richard K., and Donald Capps, eds. *On Losing the Soul: Essays in the Social Psychology of Religion.* Albany: State University of New York Press, 1995.

Greenberg, Jay R., and Stephen A. Mitchell. *Object Relations in Psychoanalytic Theory.* Cambridge: Harvard University Press, 1983.

Hawkins, Anne Hunsaker. "St. Augustine: Archetypes of Family." In *The Hunger of the Heart: Reflections on the 'Confessions' of Augustine,* edited by Donald Capps and James Dittes, 237–54. West Lafayette, Ind.: Society for the Scientific Study of Religion, 1990.

Hess, Carol Lakey. "Abomination and Creativity: Shaking the Order of the Cosmos." *Princeton Seminary Bulletin* 15, no. 1 (1994): 28–43.

Jacobs, Janet Liebman, and Donald Capps, eds. *Religion, Society, and Psychoanalysis: Readings in Contemporary Theory.* Boulder: Westview Press, 1997.

Johnson, Dirk. "When Money Is Everything, Except Hers." *New York Times,* 14 October 1998, 1A.

Jones, Ernest. *The Life and Work of Sigmund Freud, Vol. I.* New York: Basic Books, 1953.

Jones, James W. "Playing and Believing: The Uses of D. W. Winnicott in the Psychology of Religion." In *Religion, Society, and Psychoanalysis: Readings in Contemporary Theory,* edited by Janet Liebman Jacobs and Donald Capps, 106–26. Boulder: Westview Press, 1997.

Kahn, M. Masud R. "Introduction." In *Holding and Interpretation: Fragment of an Analysis,* D. W. Winnicott, 1–18. New York: Grove Press, 1986a.

Kahr, Brett. *D. W. Winnicott: A Biographical Portrait.* Madison, Conn.: International Universities Press, 1996.

Keller, Evelyn Fox. *A Feeling for the Organism: The Life and Work of Barbara McClintock.* New York: W. H. Freeman, 1983.

Koestler, Arthur. *Insight and Outlook.* Lincoln: University of Nebraska Press, 1949.

Kohut, Heinz. *The Analysis of the Self: A Systematic Approach to the Psychoanalytic Treatment of Narcissistic Personality Disorders.* Monograph No. 4, *The Psychoanalytic Study of the Child,* edited by Ruth S. Eissler et al. New York: International Universities Press, 1971.

Kolata, Gina. "Dr. Barbara McClintock, 90, Gene Research Pioneer, Dies." *New York Times,* 4 September 1992, 1A.

Kristeva, Julia. *Strangers to Ourselves.* Translated by Leon S. Roudiez. New York: Columbia University Press, 1991.

Lakoff, G., and M. Johnson. *Metaphors We Live By.* Chicago: University of Chicago Press, 1980.

Lansky, Melvin R., ed. *Essential Papers on Dreams.* New York: New York University Press, 1992.

Lewin, Bertram D. "Dream Psychology and the Analytic Situation." In *Essential Papers on Dreams,* edited by Melvin

R. Lansky, 53–77. New York: New York University Press, 1992.

Long, Thomas G. *The Witness of Preaching.* Louisville: Westminster/John Knox Press, 1989.

Luhrmann, T. M. *Of Two Minds: The Growing Disorder in American Psychiatry.* New York: Alfred A. Knopf, 2000.

Lynd, Helen Merrell. *On Shame and the Search for Identity.* New York: Harcourt Brace, 1958.

McDargh, John. "Desire, Domination, and the Life and Death of the Soul." In *On Losing the Soul: Essays in the Social Psychology of Religion,* edited by Richard K. Fenn and Donald Capps, 213–30. Albany: State University of New York Press, 1995.

McNeill, John T., and Helena M. Gamer. *Medieval Handbooks of Penance.* New York: Octagon Books, 1965.

Martin, Luther H., Huck Gutman, and Patrick H. Hutton, eds. *Technologies of the Self: A Seminar with Michel Foucault.* Amherst: University of Massachusetts Press, 1988.

Moltmann, Jürgen. *God in Creation: A New Theology of Creation and the Spirit of God.* Translated by Margaret Kohl. San Francisco: Harper & Row, 1985.

———. *The Future of Creation: Collected Essays.* Translated by Margaret Kohl. Philadelphia: Fortress Press, 1979.

Moyers, Bill. *Facing Evil.* PBS Videotape, 1988. KERA, Dallas-Fort Worth, Denton, and Public Affairs Television. Pacific Arts Video Publishing, 50 N. La Cienega Blvd., Beverly Hills, CA 90211.

Muller, Wayne. *Sabbath: Restoring the Sacred Rhythm of Rest.* New York: Bantam Books, 1999.

Nichols, J. Randall. *The Restoring Word: Preaching as Pastoral Communication.* San Francisco: Harper & Row, 1987.

Phillips, Adam. *The Beast in the Nursery: On Curiosity and Other Appetites.* New York: Pantheon Books, 1998.

———. *On Flirtation: Psychoanalytic Essays on the Uncommitted Life.* Cambridge: Harvard University Press, 1994.

———. *On Kissing, Tickling, and Being Bored: Psychoanalytic Essays on the Unexamined Life.* Cambridge: Harvard University Press, 1993.

———. *Winnicott.* Cambridge: Harvard University Press, 1988.

Pitt-Watson, Ian. *Preaching: A Kind of Folly.* Philadelphia: Westminster Press, 1976.

Porte, Joel. *Emerson in His Journals.* Cambridge: Harvard University Press, 1982.

Richardson, Jr., Robert D. *Emerson: The Mind on Fire.* Berkeley: University of California Press, 1995.

Rimer, Sara. "A Shy Scholar Transforms Dartmouth into a Haven for Intellectuals." *New York Times,* 4 January 1997, 6A.

Roberson, Susan L. *Emerson in His Sermons: A Man-Made Self.* Columbia: University of Missouri Press, 1995.

Stafford, William. *An Oregon Message.* New York: Harper & Row, 1987.

———. *You Must Revise Your Life.* Ann Arbor: University of Michigan Press, 1986.

Taylor, Gardner C. *How Shall They Preach: The Lyman Beecher Lectures and Five Lenten Sermons.* Elgin, Ill.: Progressive Baptist Publishing House, 1977.

Westendorf, Omer. "Finest Wheat." In *The Presbyterian Hymnal: Hymns, Psalms, and Spiritual Songs.* Louisville: Westminster/John Knox Press, 1990.

Winnicott, D. W. *Holding and Interpretation: Fragment of an Analysis.* New York: Grove Press, 1986a.

———. *Home Is Where We Start From: Essays by a Psychoanalyst.* New York: W. W. Norton, 1986b.

———. *The Maturational Processes and the Facilitating Environment: Studies in the Theory of Emotional Development.* Madison, Conn.: International Universities Press, 1965.

———. *Playing and Reality.* New York: Routledge, 1992.

———. *Thinking About Children.* Edited by Ray Shepherd, Jennifer Johns, and Helen Taylor Robinson. Reading, Mass.: Addison-Wesley Publishing, 1996.

———. *Through Paediatrics to Psychoanalysis.* London: Hogarth Press, 1975.

Zilboorg, Gregory. "Some Sidelights on Free Association." *International Journal of Psychoanalysis* 33 (1952): 489–95.

Index